Faithful to the Earth

Faithful to the Earth

Nietzsche and Whitehead on God and the Meaning of Human Life

J. Thomas Howe

ROWMAN & LITTLEFIELD PUBLISHERS, INC.
Lanham • *Boulder* • *New York* • *Oxford*

ROWMAN & LITTLEFIELD PUBLISHERS, INC.

Published in the United States of America
by Rowman & Littlefield Publishers, Inc.
A Member of the Rowman & Littlefield Publishing Group
4720 Boston Way, Lanham, Maryland 20706
www.rowmanlittlefield.com

PO Box 317
Oxford
OX2 9RU, UK

British Library Cataloguing in Publication Information Available

Library of Congress Cataloging-in-Publication Data

Howe, J. Thomas, 1967—
    Faithful to the earth : Nietzsche and Whitehead on God and the meaning of
human life / J. Thomas Howe.
        p. cm.
    Includes bibliographical references and index.
    ISBN 0-7425-1444-7 (hardcover : alk. paper)—ISBN 0-7425-1445-5 (pbk. : alk.
paper)
        1. Nietzsche, Friedrich Wihelm, 1844—1900. 2. Whitehead, Alfred North, 1861—
1947. 3. God—History of doctrines. 4. Meaning (Philosophy)—History. 5. Life—
History. 6. Nihilism (Philosophy)—History. I. Title.
    B3318.R4H69 2003
    211'.092'2—dc21   2002009696

Printed in the United States of America

♾™ The paper used in this publication meets the minimum requirements of
American National Standard for Information Sciences—Permanence of Paper
for Printed Library Materials, ANSI/NISO Z39.48-1992.

Contents

Abbreviations

WORKS BY NIETZSCHE

A   *The Antichrist.* In *The Portable Nietzsche.* Translated and edited by Walter Kaufmann. New York: Penguin, 1982.

BGE   *Beyond Good and Evil.* Translated by Walter Kaufmann. New York: Vintage, 1966.

BT   *The Birth of Tragedy.* In *The Birth of Tragedy and The Case of Wagner.* Translated by Walter Kaufmann. New York: Vintage, 1967.

CW   *The Case of Wagner.* In *The Birth of Tragedy and The Case of Wagner.* Translated by Walter Kaufmann. New York: Vintage, 1967.

D   *Daybreak.* Translated by R. J. Hollingdale. Cambridge: Cambridge University Press, 1982.

DS   *David Strauss the Confessor and the Writer.* In *Unfashionable Observations.* Translated by Richard T. Gray. Stanford, Calif.: Stanford University Press, 1995.

EH   *Ecce Homo.* In *On the Genealogy of Morals and Ecce Homo.* Translated by Walter Kaufmann. New York: Vintage, 1974.

GM   *On the Genealogy of Morals.* In *On the Genealogy of Morals and Ecce Homo.* Translated by Walter Kaufmann. New York: Vintage, 1974.

GS   *The Gay Science.* Translated by Walter Kaufmann. New York: Vintage, 1974.

HATH   *Human, All Too Human.* Translated by Gary Handwerk. Stanford, Calif.: Stanford University Press, 1997.

RWB   *Richard Wagner in Bayreuth.* In *Unfashionable Observations.* Translated by Richard T. Gray. Stanford, Calif.: Stanford University Press, 1995.

SE   *Schopenhauer as Educator.* In *Unfashionable Observations.* Translated by Richard T. Gray. Stanford, Calif.: Stanford University Press, 1995.

TI   *Twilight of the Idols.* In *The Portable Nietzsche.* Translated and edited by Walter Kaufmann. New York: Penguin, 1982.

TL   *On Truth and Lie in an Extra-Moral Sense.* In *The Portable Nietzsche.* Translated and edited by Walter Kaufmann. New York: Penguin, 1982.

ULH   *The Utility and Liability of History.* In *Unfashionable Observations.* Translated by Richard T. Gray. Stanford, Calif.: Stanford University Press, 1995.

WP   *The Will to Power.* Translated by Walter Kaufmann and R. J. Hollingdale. New York: Vintage, 1968.

Z   *Thus Spoke Zarathustra.* In *The Portable Nietzsche.* Translated and edited by Walter Kaufmann. New York: Penguin, 1982.

Most references to Nietzsche's works cite the abbreviation and the aphorism or section number. References to *Thus Spoke Zarathustra, On the Genealogy of Morals, The Twilight of the Idols,* and *Ecce Homo* cite the abbreviation, chapter number or name, and section number. In the case of *On Truth and Lie in an Extra-Moral Sense,* I cite the abbreviation and the page number in *The Portable Nietzsche.*

WORKS BY WHITEHEAD

AI   *Adventures of Ideas*. New York: Free Press, 1967.

DLG   *Dialogues of Alfred North Whitehead*. Recorded and edited by Lucien Price. Boston: Little, Brown, 1954.

FR   *The Function of Reason*. Boston: Beacon, 1929.

IMM   "Immortality." In *Science and Philosophy*. New York: Philosophical Library, 1974.

MG   "Mathematics and the Good." In *Science and Philosophy*. New York: Philosophical Library, 1974.

MT   *Modes of Thought*. New York: Free Press, 1968.

PR   *Process and Reality*, corrected edition, edited by David Ray Griffin and Donald W. Sherburne. New York: Free Press, 1978.

RM   *Religion in the Making*. New York: Fordham University Press, 1996.

S   *Symbolism*. New York: Fordham University Press, 1985.

SMW   *Science and the Modern World*. New York: Free Press, 1967.

SP   *Science and Philosophy*. New York: Philosophical Library, 1974.

References to Whitehead's works cite the abbreviation and the page number.

Acknowledgments

Throughout my education, I have been blessed with exceptional teachers. This fortune was greatly exemplified by my teachers at Claremont Graduate University, where this book began as a dissertation some time ago. Without the guidance of my dissertation committee, my thoughts on the matters discussed in these pages would have remained undoubtedly in a state of romantic confusion. Anybody who has worked with David Griffin will know how much of him is in this study. If it were not for his passion, generosity with ideas and time, and patience, my engagement with the philosophy of Whitehead would have lasted but a moment. Tad Beckman, from Harvey Mudd College, provided a great deal of help with the sections on Nietzsche. Steve Smith, from Claremont McKenna College, delivered insights available only to one who has pledged allegiance neither to Whitehead nor Nietzsche. I am grateful to the three of them. Thanks are due also to Kathryn Hutchinson for reading and commenting on a draft of the original dissertation.

Jim Tselepis taught me how to spell Nietzsche when we were both freshman in college, thereby enabling me to avoid a certain shame. But more important, he graced the manuscript by sharing his poetic understanding of language and correcting an embarrassing number of grammatical errors.

Many of the general questions and issues raised in this study were initially introduced to me by my first teacher of religion, Ronald Miller of Lake Forest College. I am grateful for his help and friendship, which have continued to this day.

Finally, in many ways, this book is about world-views—some problematic, others more hopeful. Much more than gratitude needs to be expressed to Nancy Christmas, my wife, who knows more about vision than anyone I know and spends her days promoting good world-views.

1

Introduction

This book is a comparison of Friedrich Nietzsche and Alfred North Whitehead on a cluster of questions and topics encompassing the relationship between God and the meaning of human life in the world. On the surface, Nietzsche and Whitehead represent very different positions in regard to these questions and topics. Quite simply, Nietzsche argues with great passion that belief in the Christian God amounts to a denial of the value and meaning of human life in the world. In contrast, for Whitehead, human life can find no meaning unless God exists, most notably a God that resembles the God of Christianity. Although the differences between an atheist and a theist make comparative study possible, if there are merely these surface differences, the comparison either has difficulty in moving beyond the simple display of differences or engages in some sort of dogmatic and monological polemic. In other words, if it were simply the case that Nietzsche is an atheist and Whitehead a theist, in the sense that these terms are simple opposites, this comparison would be relatively uninteresting. But bringing Whitehead and Nietzsche together provides more opportunities than simple contrast. A number of provocative and fruitful proposals about the relationship between God and the meaning of human life emerge when one comes to a deeper understanding of the views of Nietzsche and Whitehead. These possibilities are due to the fact that both Nietzsche and Whitehead are "philosophers of process,"[1] meaning that for Nietzsche and Whitehead, reality is best described as a "process" or a "process of

1

becoming." Nietzsche's criticism of Christianity is based on this presupposition, just as Whitehead's theism is also based on it.

At the heart of this book is the following question: What are the implications of finitude and transience for the meaningfulness of human life? The finite and transient nature of human existence seems to present a real threat to the possibility that life is meaningful: achievements are forgotten, pleasures fade, friendships are lost, and physical life always comes to an end. We live in a world where, in the words of Elizabeth Bishop, "It's evident the art of losing's not too hard to master."[2] And in words attributed to Solomon: "For of the wise man as of the fool there is no enduring remembrance, seeing that in the days to come all will have been long forgotten. How the wise man dies just like the fool!"[3] The passage of time brings everything, the good and the bad, to an end.

The finitude of existence is particularly distressing because meaningfulness has long been associated with the long-lasting, if not the outright, eternal. Consider the description of "true love" given by Shakespeare in one of his sonnets:

> Let me not to the marriage of true minds
> Admit impediments. Love is not love
> Which alters when it alteration finds,
> Or bends with the remover to remove.
> O no, it is an ever fixed mark
> . . . . Love's not time's fool.[4]

But, of course, the immediate problem is whether or not "an ever fixed mark" actually exists, and if there is anything that is "not time's fool." Are transience and finitude the whole story? Are we limited to the fleeting pleasures of the Vanity Fair? Or, is there something more? Do actions, achievements, failures, and the like, have any real significance? Dealing with these questions has long been the business of philosophy and religion, and answers have varied greatly in style, tone, and content. One of the more prominent answers within Western thought has been to state that in some way change and transience are not the marks of the really real. What is really real is that which does not change. And, although finitude, transience, and becoming may seem ubiquitous, these qualities are, in some sense or another, the marks of appearance, of something ultimately unreal, or something not worthy of human veneration. Within Western philosophical and religious thought, one finds various expressions of some sort of "ever fixed mark."

We find one of the most influential articulations of the presupposition that Being is more real than Becoming in the thoughts of Plato and Socrates. In the *Phaedo*, Plato recounts the final hours of Socrates' life. Socrates is trying to convince his friends that his impending execution is nothing to fear and that he has really been preparing for this moment his entire life. "True philosophers," he says, "make dying their profession, and that to them of all men death is least alarming."[5] Death is nothing more than the separation of the body from the soul. And because the philosopher is far more interested in the life of the soul than the body, death is a gateway to a better existence.

But what makes the life of the soul worthy of philosophical interest? The answer to this question reveals Plato's and Socrates' presupposition that what is really real is that which does not change. Philosophers, Socrates says, are interested in truth. And truth is that which is not subject to variation but is eternal and unchanging. The body makes the pursuit of truth difficult because it has access only to the world of variation and change. Furthermore, the body's instruments are prone to error. Socrates advocates a life devoted to the soul, with the advantage being that one no longer traffics in the unreliable world of change and begins to acquire access to a world of eternal and unchanging ideas.

The philosophy of Plato and his followers proved favorable to many early Christian theologians. One of the most influential of these theologians was St. Augustine, who accepted and made great use of the idea that the permanent and eternal are more real than the transient. He writes, "I had realized that what is incorruptible is better than that which is not."[6] That which is best is God, for God is absolutely immutable and incorruptible. God's perfection and eminence reside in the fact that God does not *suffer* change. In contrast to God, human life in the world is wrought with change (which Augustine usually equates with decay); for this reason, life has a tragic quality to it. Human beings live in an unstable world where eventually everything comes to an end. Augustine believed that the transient nature of all worldly events and entities makes it entirely difficult to find something dependable on which a life can be grounded. All devotion and attachment to worldly entities will leave one, at some moment or another, wanting. *The Confessions*, Augustine's autobiography, is largely a book that tells of his failed attempts to find meaning in wholly worldly and transient entities. The great climax of the book is his conversion to Christianity. Just prior to this event he writes that he was in a state of despair and indecision. Tired of his present lifestyle yet unable to devote himself to God, Augustine was in dire straits. "I was in torment, reproaching myself more bitterly than ever as I twisted and turned in my chain. I hoped that my chain might be broken once and for all."[7] Augustine's inner life was in chaos as he attempted to serve what seemed to be two conflicting wills. Upon his conversion, Augustine experiences a sense of peace. "For in the instant . . . it was as though the light of confidence flooded into my heart and all the darkness of doubt was dispelled."[8] The contrast between Augustine's religious life and his secular life is one of the differences between a life of peace and coherence and a life of turmoil and chaos. God provides Augustine with the foundation by which life in the world of transience and chaos can be endured; Augustine discovers that this world is grounded by something incorruptible.

Augustine poignantly articulates the apparent tragedy involved in worldly life and the possibility of overcoming tragedy by means of a life rooted in God when he recounts the death of his dear friend from Thagaste: "I lived in misery, like every man whose soul is tethered by the love of things that cannot last and then is agonized to lose them."[9] His misery is due to his attachment to his friend. Thus, when his friend is lost, so, too, he thinks, is all of the value Augustine had derived from the relationship. This experience leads Augustine to the conclusion that life in a wholly transient world is a gloomy affair, for no relationship to things we find valuable can be sustained. But if we turn our desire to God, the eternal nature of God makes it possible to love something that is not subject to decay, something that will not fail with the passage of time. "Blessed are those who love you O God, and love their friends in you. . . . They alone will never lose those who are dear to them, for they love them in one who is never lost, in God, our God."[10] For Augustine, the way to live in the world is to be devoted to an object that is outside the realm of finitude. This is not to say that one must completely abandon this world, but that we are to love the world only insofar as it reflects God. At this point, we can come to an appreciation of Augustine's often quoted comment that "our hearts find no peace until they rest in [God]."[11]

For Plato and Augustine, transience and finitude are thought to be the sources of discord. For them and many who follow, finitude is a problem and a threat to the meaning and value of human life. For Augustine, the tragic quality of life in a finite and transient world is overcome by coming to know that God provides a rock-solid foundation and that a life of loving God will not go unrequited. For Plato and Socrates, we can avoid the problem of finitude by turning inward, cultivating a life of the soul, which is not finite. So great was the idea that the permanent and eternal are ontologically superior to the transient that the formation of orthodox Christian theology was governed by the axiom that God is absolutely immutable. In no substantial way whatsoever could one attribute any sort of Becoming to God.[12]

Much of our discussion of Nietzsche and Whitehead will revolve around their respective critical responses to these sorts of strategies for dealing with the presumed problem of finitude. A good portion of Nietzsche's philosophical work is devoted to showing that what he calls the "True World of Being" does not exist, and that the desire that there is something beyond this world of Becoming is wishful (and harmful) thinking. Whitehead's major work is entitled *Process and Reality*, which implies that *reality is process*. Recounting his views of Hegel and Bradley, Whitehead writes, "I differ from them where they all agree in their feeling of the illusiveness and relative unreality of the temporal world" (*SP*, 124).

Does this mean, then, that if Nietzsche and Whitehead are correct we are left with a world that will forever disappoint? To be sure, it is true that Nietzsche claims that "God is dead"—which means that the suprasensible realm of static Being is no longer believable. And with the demise of God, so, too, go many of the values that have been at the core of idea that life is meaningful. Nietzsche has been so adamant about these issues, and his comments have been particularly eristic, that he is often understood to be an "existential nihilist," as one who claims that human life is without meaning. Whitehead, too, though to a far lesser degree, has written about the downfall of the traditional doctrine of God and the consequences of these events.

But neither Whitehead nor Nietzsche accepts these circumstances as lamentable facts. Rather, they present new opportunities. The desire for, and effort toward achieving, the sort of stability granted by the view that Being is ontologically superior to Becoming requires, think both Nietzsche and Whitehead, that one withdraw from activities in the world and relationships with others. A new appreciation for the reality of Becoming makes possible a new affirmation of worldly life. "Remain faithful to the earth," Nietzsche has Zarathustra say (*Z*, prologue, 3). Furthermore, the quality and profundity of experience are increased, both Nietzsche and Whitehead argue, by an acceptance of the reality of finitude. In fact, we could say that finitude is the condition for the possibility of meaningful experience.

For Nietzsche, the death of God brings about the possibility for a new interpretation of the meaning of human life in the world. In short, it allows for a newfound (or rediscovered) sense of innocence. With some rhetorical flair, Nietzsche states that the antichrist is the antinihilist (*GM*, II:24). The traditional presupposition that Being is more real than Becoming serves as a judge over, and devaluation of human life as it exists in a world of change. If static Being is the mark of ultimate reality, then life in a world of Becoming can only be construed as less than real. Therefore, if we can show that the static world of Being, or what Nietzsche calls the "metaphysical world," does not exist, we no longer need to think that finitude and transience, or what we can call the qualities of Becoming, are the marks of inferiority. But Nietzsche's hope for a new innocence does not sink in as easily as it might seem, for we are still left with a world where everything perishes. Nietzsche often described his philosophy as "tragic." In the pages that follow, we will see what this tragic philosophy entails.

I said in the opening paragraph that Whitehead is a theist. Yet, if he is a process thinker, it seems that his theism is in contradiction with his basic view that process and Becoming are more real than Being and permanence. This would be true if Whitehead's doctrine of God retained the idea that God is wholly permanent and immutable. But Whitehead's understanding of God is worked out in a way that is wholly consistent with his presupposition that process is real. Whitehead's God is a God of process and change. It is this fact that provides, I think, the most interesting prospect for a dialogue between Whitehead and Nietzsche. Whitehead's understanding of God emerges out of a criticism of the classical doctrine of God that shares much in common with Nietzsche's. The traditional doctrine of God, Whitehead argues, makes it impossible to give any significant meaning or value to the world in which we live. This problem is due to a

conceptual logic that construes *permanence* and *flux* to be wholly antithetical to one another. God is thought to be wholly permanent,
whereas the world is understood as entirely fluent. As such, because
God is given the status of eminent reality, the religious drive is to forsake the value of the world of flux and all that it entails, resulting in
what Charles Hartshorne calls "ontolatry,"[13] the worship of Being.
But, unlike Nietzsche, Whitehead does not think that this criticism requires an abandonment of the Christian idea of God altogether.
Rather, it provides the opportunity for a different understanding of
God. Hartshorne writes, "It is not clear that [Nietzsche's] objection applies to all ideas about God."[14] For Whitehead, God is not a statically
permanent entity. Rather, like worldly entities, God is in process.

One argument of this study is that Whitehead's thought provides a
doctrine of God that is not subject to most of Nietzsche's criticism of
Christianity; this doctrine is, I think, *faithful to the earth*, speaking not
of vain otherworldly hopes. Furthermore, it provides the foundation
for a religious life that has much in common with Nietzsche's view of
the tragic life. Religious life, for Whitehead is not at all opposed to life
in the world. Rather, it is a life of eros that forever seeks, attains, and
desires yet again ever-new forms of beauty. Having said this, some
caution is necessary. In the end, we will not have made Nietzsche into
a process theologian, nor will Whitehead become the antichrist, or
even Zarathustra. There remain some important differences.

The biggest difference is that Whitehead's doctrine of God does
provide an answer to the problem of "perpetual perishing" in that
God retains everlastingly all of the values achieved in the world. But
this difference does not, I argue, put Whitehead's theism in the same
camp that Nietzsche criticized. The issue at stake is the status of the
finite world. Nietzsche was weary of schemes that promised otherworldly delights at the expense of the finite world. Whitehead's answer to the problem of perpetual perishing does not decrease the status of the finite and its intrinsic value.

PREVIOUS STUDIES OF NIETZSCHE AND WHITEHEAD

Despite the great potential for dialogue, very little work has been done
on Nietzsche and Whitehead together. For the most part, commentators have been content to make passing remarks on some parallel or

another. In a section of W. T. Jones's chapter on Whitehead in his *History of Western Philosophy*, entitled "Criticism of the Dominant Philosophical Scheme," he writes that "in one respect Whitehead was perhaps closer to Nietzsche than to any of the nineteenth-century philosophers."[15] In his *What Nietzsche Means*, George Morgan puts Whitehead in a list of thinkers who are "in some way spiritually akin" to Nietzsche.[16] Walter Kaufmann suggests, in passing, that Nietzsche's concept "of a vast plurality of individual wills to power" culminates in a "monodological pluralism that shows interesting parallels to that of Whitehead."[17] But a comparison is not taken up because it "would take us too far afield."[18] There are two essays that compare Nietzsche and Whitehead on particular topics. Strachan Donnelley's essay "Whitehead and Nietzsche: Overcoming the Evil of Time" compares Nietzsche's view of the problem of time, according to which it creates burdens from the past that are difficult to overcome, with Whitehead's contrary notion that "temporal process inevitably destroys worldly achievements."[19] Forest Wood's "Creativity, Whitehead, and Nietzsche" argues that "Whitehead's view that the world is a creative advance into novelty is compatible with Nietzsche's creative overman."[20]

One of the biggest reasons for the lack of any full-length study dealing with Nietzsche and Whitehead probably involves the differences in orientations and backgrounds of their respective commentators and followers. On the one hand, Nietzsche scholars and Nietzsche-inspired philosophers show little interest in or even are hostile toward Whitehead's overall purpose, which was to develop a metaphysical philosophy that unites scientific and humanistic concerns. An antimetaphysical bias initiated by aspects of Nietzsche's writings, continued by Heidegger, and supported by Wittgenstein, has been at the foundation of most of American philosophy departments. Furthermore, Whitehead's thought has had its greatest impact on American theology, an area of discourse rarely appealing to Nietzscheans.

On the other hand, the majority of Whiteheadian-inspired philosophers has generally not looked at Nietzsche in depth. For example, although David Griffin has persuasively argued for the crucial importance of process thought for a truly "constructive postmodern philosophy" that transcends the problems of modernity, Nietzsche figures only as the precursor to the "deconstructive" thinkers who Griffin finds to be more ultramodern than postmodern.[21]

Another reason for the neglect is surely the fact that Whitehead's published writings give only scant evidence that he had read or even thought about Nietzsche. Nietzsche is mentioned only once, and here Whitehead accuses him of "anti-intellectualism" (*AI*, 223). In the collection of "dialogues" with Whitehead published by Lucien Price, there are accounts of two discussions where Nietzsche is mentioned. But in the first, Price asks Whitehead whether he has read Nietzsche's *Antichrist*, to which Whitehead promptly responds, "No" (*DLG*, 134). In the second, Price mentions Nietzsche's observation that "suffering may deepen a man" (*DLG*, 167). Whitehead takes up a discussion of anxiety and how it sharpens one's impressions, but he does not follow with any discussion of Nietzsche.

Before coming to America, Whitehead, it seems, would have had little opportunity to encounter Nietzsche's writings. Nietzsche received only scant attention in England in the 1890s. Until 1903 only three volumes of Nietzsche's works had been translated into English.[22] Whitehead evidently was exposed to Nietzsche while at Harvard, but probably only when his writing days were coming to an end. In the preface of *What Nietzsche Means*, published in 1941, George Morgan thanks Whitehead "for much counsel throughout, concerning both the form and content of this study."[23]

NOTES

1. Nietzsche would fail to qualify for inclusion within David Griffin's formal definition of a "process philosopher" given that he defines "process philosophy" as "that movement initiated by Alfred North Whitehead (1861–1947) and Charles Hartshorne (1897[–1999])." But it is more than an anachronism that keeps Nietzsche off the list. Griffin's formal, limited definition also includes ten criteria, many of which Nietzsche would not fulfill. It is not my intention to appeal this exclusion, nor is it really necessary. In a wider sense, "process philosophy," writes Griffin, "can legitimately be used quite broadly to refer to a wide range of positions emphasizing the ultimate reality of becoming, process, and change" (see David Ray Griffin, *Reenchantment without Supernaturalism: A Process Philosophy of Religion* [Ithaca, N.Y.: Cornell University Press, 2001], 1–2). Nietzsche does adhere to this basic presupposition, and it is for this reason that dialogue between Nietzsche and Whitehead is possible.

2. Elizabeth Bishop, "One Art," in *The Complete Poems 1927–1979* (New York: Farrar, Straus & Giroux, 1979).

3. Ecclesiastes 2:16.

4. William Shakespeare, *Shakespeare's Sonnets*, ed. Stanley Wells (Oxford: Oxford University Press, 1985), 130.

5. Plato, *Phaedo* in *The Collected Dialogues*, ed. Edith Hamilton and Huntington Cairns (Princeton, N.J.: Princeton University Press, 1961), section 67C.

6. St. Augustine, *The Confessions*, trans. R. S. Pine Coffin (New York: Penguin, 1961), Book VII, section 7.

7. Augustine, Book VII, section 7.

8. Augustine, Book VIII, section 12.

9. Augustine, Book IV, section 6.

10. Augustine, Book IV, section, 9.

11. Augustine, Book I, section 1.

12. Subsequently, the formative stages of orthodox theology were required to uphold this axiom. This allegiance caused innumerable conceptual problems when attempts were made to interpret various Scriptures and to form the doctrines of the Trinity and the Incarnation. Jaroslav Pelikan writes that when the Alexandrian theologians attempted to interpret Psalm 94, with its statement that God *becomes* man's refuge, they were required to state that "the very mention of the word 'God' made the interpretation of 'become' as applied to God 'stupid and altogether wicked' if it is supposed that this could refer to any sort of change in the unchangeable God" (*The Christian Tradition: A History of the Development of Doctrine*, vol. 1: *The Emergence of the Catholic Tradition (100–600)* [Chicago: University of Chicago Press, 1971], 230).

13. Charles Hartshorne and William Reese, *Philosophers Speak of God* (New York: Humanity, 2000), 24.

14. Hartshorne and Reese, *Philosophers Speak of God,* 468.

15. W. T. Jones, *History of Western Philosophy*, vol. 5, *The Twentieth Century to Wittgenstein and Sartre* (New York: Harcourt Brace Jovanovich, 1975), 71.

16. George Morgan, *What Nietzsche Means* (New York: Harper Torchbooks, 1941), 6.

17. Walter Kaufmann, *Nietzsche: Philosopher, Psychologist, Antichrist,* 4th ed. (Princeton, N.J.: Princeton University Press, 1974), 243.

18. Kaufmann, *Nietzsche,* 243.

19. Strachan Donnelley, "Whitehead and Nietzsche: Overcoming the Evil of Time," *Process Studies* 12:1 (Spring 1982): p. 1.

20. Forest Wood, "Creativity: Whitehead, and Nietzsche," *Southwest Philosophical Studies* 9:2 (Winter 1983): p. 58.

21. David Ray Griffin, "Introduction to SUNY Series in Constructive Postmodern Thought," in *Founders of Constructive Postmodern Philosophy: Pierce, James, Bergson, Whitehead, and Hartshorne*, ed. David Ray Griffin (Albany: State University of New York Press, 1993).

22. David S. Thatcher, *Nietzsche in England 1890–1914* (Toronto: University of Toronto Press, 1970), 36.

23. Morgan, *What Nietzsche Means*, viii–ix.

2

The Death of God
and the Problem of Nihilism

In this chapter, I begin my discussion of Nietzsche's criticism of Christianity. Throughout his entire life, Nietzsche was exercised and, at time, fascinated by Christ, Christians, and Christianity. These interests are reflected in virtually all of Nietzsche's writings. Even in his first published work, *The Birth of Tragedy*, where Christianity goes unmentioned, Nietzsche wrote in a preface added fourteen years after its initial publication, "In truth nothing could be more opposed to the purely aesthetic interpretation and justification of the world which are taught in this book than the Christian teaching, which is, and wants to be, *only* moral" (*BT*, "Attempt at a Self-Criticism," 5). Although Nietzsche occasionally articulated an admiration for certain aspects of Christianity, especially the person of Jesus Christ, his attitude was predominantly critical, and usually this criticism had a polemical tone. Even his praises are loaded with reservations. For Nietzsche, the worldview and values of Christianity are unable to sustain and cultivate a meaningful human existence.

Nietzsche wavers between two different answers when faced with the question of why and how Christianity fails in this regard. In the first place, he claims that the Christian God and the values it supports are no longer believable. God is, as Nietzsche is famous for saying, *dead*. In this case, Nietzsche is diagnosing what he sees as the contemporary cultural situation. Due to contemporary trends in science (e.g., Darwinism) and historical studies (e.g., the historical-critical study of the Bible), the Christian God is no longer believable. When thinking in this way, Nietzsche often takes the attitude that something catastrophic has happened and that something of great importance has been lost. But in the second place, Nietzsche takes a different stance. Frequently, he treats Christianity as something alive, flourishing, and exerting a great deal of influence. No longer writing as one who is merely chronicling the death of God, Nietzsche writes with the intention of serving as a catalyst to the demise of humanity's belief in God. Nietzsche's goal is to expose Christianity and Christians as "decadent." The Christian worldview is, he thinks, the production of weakness, *ressentiment*, and an inability to affirm worldly human life. These two views, as I will explain, are not unrelated.

THE BREATH OF HISTORY AND THE DEATH OF GOD

> How weary, stale, flat, and unprofitable
> Seem to me all the uses of this world!
> Fie on't, ah fie! 'Tis an unweeded garden
> That grows to seed.
>
> —*William Shakespeare*, Hamlet

In the mid-1880s, Nietzsche noticed that the "uncanniest of all guests," nihilism, was standing at the door of European society (*WP*, 1; 1885–1886).[1] The term *nihilism* appears frequently in Nietzsche's writings, often with different adjectival modifications.[2] Common to these different uses of the term is a reference to a sense of the futility and meaninglessness of human life in the world. Nihilism means, he says, "the aim is lacking; 'why?' finds no answer" (*WP*, 2; 1887). This feeling of nihilism was quickly spreading throughout European civilization and would soon reach, Nietzsche thought, catastrophic proportions.

> For some time now, our whole European culture has been moving as toward a catastrophe, with a tortured tension that is growing from decade to decade: restlessly, violently, headlong, like a river that wants to reach the end, that no longer reflects, that is afraid to reflect. (*WP*, preface, 2; 1887–1888)

The result of this catastrophe will be a culture that no longer has any reverence for human life in the world. Nietzsche wanted, as

George Morgan states, "to understand and evaluate this plight, to detect its cause and foresee its possible outcome, and, thus grounded to build toward a future civilization with a more adequate philosophy."[3] From his earliest published writings to the last, and throughout a lifetime of unpublished notebooks, Nietzsche's philosophy represents an engagement with the problem of nihilism.[4]

Nietzsche was beginning to see that much of the Western tradition and its ways of construing the meaning of human life was based on a faulty and quickly disintegrating foundation. Like so many others in the nineteenth century, Nietzsche was becoming acutely aware of the radically transient and ephemeral nature of existence.[5] In 1876, he wrote:

> In and of itself no event is great, even if entire constellations disappear, nations perish, vast states are founded, and wars are waged with tremendous forces and tremendous losses; the breath of history has blown away many such things as though they were nothing but snowflakes. (*RWB*, 1)

Confronted with the experience of the sheer temporal and contingent nature of existence or, to use a phrase of Milan Kundera, the "lightness of being,"[6] Nietzsche was faced with sorting out the implications of this experience for the traditional metaphysical and religious understandings of reality. His sense was that the discovery of the radically historical nature of reality would have magnificent and awesome repercussions.

The most significant of these repercussions is the death of God. Prior to this point, Nietzsche states that human beings widely used three supports, or foundations, by which they could view human life in the world as meaningful. These foundations served the function of allowing humanity to make sense of the apparent transience and finitude of human life in the world. First, there was the belief that human life and the world were moving toward some teleological aim, or final state. In this case, the meaning of life comes at the end of the process, thus justifying the process. Second, often one posited a "totality, a systematization, indeed any organization in all events, and underneath all events" (*WP*, 12; 1887–1888). This is the belief in some form of unity or monism that unites all differences and particularities. It gives us, Nietzsche writes, "a deep feeling of standing in the context of, and being dependent on, some whole that is infinitely superior to [ourselves]" (*WP*, 12; 1887–1888). Third, there was the belief that this world of Becoming was not the True World, that beyond this world existed a place not subject to the problems of this world. All three of these supports function in a manner that allows human beings to make sense of change and Becoming by grounding the transient world in something that does not change. Presupposed in all three of these supports is the idea that Becoming is less real than Being. Becoming is accidental and ultimately unreal. These supports have usually been understood as God.

However, the supposed existence of these supports was becoming dubious. The discovery of the historical nature of all of reality means that all beliefs in some metaphysical or ahistorical realm are self-created fictions. Explicating Nietzsche's view, David Michael Levin writes "as we human beings developed within our culture and became increasingly self-conscious, increasingly disposed toward self-examination, we have been compelled with a corresponding intensity and lucidity to recognize our own participation in the presence of value in our world."[7] A historical-critical audit of anything, Nietzsche writes in *The Utility and Liability of History*, destroys much of its persuasive power and presumed value.

> The reason for this is that every historical audit always brings to light so much falsehood, coarseness, inhumanity, absurdity, and violence that the pious atmosphere of illusion, in which alone everything that wants to live is actually capable of life, vanishes. (*ULH*, 7)

What was presumed to be eternal and given turns out to be historical and created by human beings. Nietzsche is reaffirming the age-old discovery of Xenophanes, who states that if horses could draw gods, these gods would look like horses.

Because God was the very foundation of European culture by which human life was made meaningful, the growing realization that everything is ephemeral and that God is dead should bring with it the despairing experience that what had previously been thought to be the Real, what one had staked one's life on, was a sham: "And how much must collapse now that this faith has been undermined because it was built upon this faith, propped up by it, grown into it" (*GS*, 343).

The death of God and the growing sense that reality is entirely historical amounts to the demise of those foundations that were presumed to support and ground the world of transience. A "True World of Being" does not, Nietzsche thinks, support the world of Becoming. He writes: "Existence has no goal or end; any comprehensive unity in the plurality of events is lacking. . . . One simply lacks any reason for convincing oneself that there is a *true* world" (*WP*, 12; 1887–1888). Blown away with the breath of history and the death of God are virtually all the ideals that have propelled and supported Western culture. The ice has "become very thin," he says, using another metaphor (*GS*, 377). Nietzsche states over and over that one is no longer entitled to the belief that nature and history are governed by reason, let alone divine reason. European morality has lost its divine sanction. The human being can no longer be construed as having "absolute" value. Above all, human misfortunes, sufferings, and other evils can no longer be thought to have justifiable explanations. The traditional religious, and even secular, theodicies no longer have any basis. About Europe's "highest values," Nietzsche writes, "that is all over now" (*GS*, 357). We must "reject the Christian interpretation and condemn its 'meaning' like counterfeit." And with this rejection, the passage continues, "*Schopenhauer's* question immediately comes to us in a terrifying way: Has existence any meaning at all?" (*GS*, 357).

THE SORROW OF KNOWLEDGE

The question then arises that if something that was once believed in is no longer believable, and this has been realized because we have become more mature and sophisticated in our understanding of the world, why would this necessarily result in a crisis and a time of despair? The trouble, Nietzsche notices, is that the truth we have come to realize does not appeal to us. The truth of "sovereign becoming, of the fluidity of all concepts, types, and species, of the lack of any cardinal difference between human and animal"—in short, the truth of the "death of God"—appears to us as "deadly" (*ULH*, 9). This truth creates, Nietzsche writes, an antagonism. "This antagonism—not to esteem what we know, and not to be allowed any longer to esteem the lies we should like to tell ourselves—results in a process of dissolution" (*WP*, 5; 1887). Because we have discovered that God is dead and that the values we gave to existence have historical origins, we no longer find them believable. But most important, we are not yet able to affirm the world as we now know it to be—as a place of incessant becoming, change, and chaos. In an aphorism entitled "Sorrow Is Knowledge,"[8] Nietzsche writes:

> How gladly we would exchange the false assertions of priests that there is a God who demands what is good from us, the watcher and witness of every action, every moment, every thought, who loves us and wants the best for us in every affliction—how gladly we would exchange all this for truths that would be just as salutary, soothing, and beneficial as those errors! Yet such truths do not exist. (*HATH*, I: 109)

We want very much to be able to align ourselves with, and live in terms of practices that are in accordance with, the truth. But the truth, now that God is dead, seems deadly. While the belief in God pacified us by enabling us to assuage a chaotic and discordant world, this peace is no longer available. "Such truths do not exist." The aphorism concludes with another description of what Nietzsche takes to be the modern condition:

> Yet the tragedy is that we cannot *believe* those dogmas of religion and metaphysics if we have the strict method of truth in our hearts and heads, but on the other hand, the development of humanity has made us so delicate, irritable, and sickly that we need remedies and consolations of the highest kind; in consequence of which, therefore, the danger arises that *humanity may bleed to death from recognizing truth*. (*HATH*, I: 109; emphasis added)

The "deadly" truth makes life seem futile. Actions and deeds seem to add up to nothing.

REACTIONS TO THE DEATH OF GOD

To be sure, Nietzsche was deeply concerned with the death of God and the potential it had for unleashing a conscious sense of despair. But what roused Nietzsche's attention even more was the fact that, for the most part, the death of God did not create a mood of anxious despair, as Nietzsche thought it should. Instead, the antagonism between what we need and what we now know about the nature of reality was greeted with either a superficial optimism, which Nietzsche calls "incomplete nihilism," or a repressive and complacent apathy, which he refers to as "passive nihilism."

David Strauss's Superficial Optimism

In some circles, the death of God was met with a response that was all too positive and optimistic about its consequences. Some of these responses did not think through carefully enough just what is involved in the death of God. It is sometimes thought that Nietzsche naïvely assumed that being liberated from the traditional views of the Real was something to be embraced lightly and optimistically. But Nietzsche knows that the death of God is serious business, and no one has taken the possibility of being stuck in the Saturday between Good Friday and Easter Sunday more gravely than Nietzsche.

In *The Gay Science*, Nietzsche tells a parable involving a madman. When this madman comes to the marketplace looking for God and announcing that God is dead, he provokes only laughter. Because the people of the marketplace think that they long ago gave up such superstitious beliefs, they take him for a fool. But after continuing to rant with a prophetic urgency and in frustration that nobody quite grasps what is happening, the madman finally falls silent. He thinks to himself, "'I have come too early . . . my time is not yet. This tremendous event is still on its way, still wandering; it has not yet reached the ears of men. . . . This deed is still more distant from them than the most distant stars'" (*GS*, 125). Although the people of the marketplace think they have accepted God's death and found suitable alternatives, their lives and practices, Nietzsche notices, do not reflect just how serious such a thing is and just how much has happened and how much must now change.

Nietzsche singles out David Strauss's *The Old and New Faith* as one of the prime exemplars of this contemporary trait. This book, he thinks, is a "beer-bench gospel," being nothing more than a narcotic that anesthetizes the consequences of the death of God with a superficial optimism (*TI*, "What the Germans Lack," 2). Nietzsche argues throughout *David Strauss the Confessor and the Writer* that Strauss thought himself to be fully modern, embracing Darwin, the views of natural science, and the serious challenges they offered to the "old faith." After explaining the impossibility of living by means of the "old faith," Strauss put forth the possibility of living a life based on a "new faith." Yet, Nietzsche contends, Strauss is far too content with this picture of the world, never fully and honestly fleshing out the ramifications of his Darwinian world.

With a certain crude contentment he covers himself with the shaggy cloak of our ape-genealogists and praises Darwin as one of humankind's greatest benefactors—but we realize with consternation that his ethics is constructed independently of the question: "How do we conceive the world?" (*DS*, 7)

Strauss, Nietzsche thinks, constructed an ethics and a view of the human being that did not correspond to his professed Darwinism. Strauss's conception of reality and his ethics are at odds with one another. Despite Strauss's excitement about Darwin, he still urged his readers never to forget that they are more than a mere creature of nature and that the essence of morality depends on this elevation of the human personality beyond the animal realm. Nietzsche asks rhetorically, "How can this [morality] be innate to human beings when, according to Darwin, the human being is wholly a creature of nature?" (*DS*, 7).

The freedom derived from exposing Christianity's mythical and historical origins is not at all as light and easy as Strauss thought it to be. If Strauss were to go the distance with Darwin, Nietzsche argues, he would have to give up both his highly esteemed view of human beings and his morality. "When one gives up the Christian faith," Nietzsche writes, "one pulls the right to Christian morality out from under one's feet" (*TI*, "Skirmishes of an Untimely Man," 5). Strauss, like those confronted by the madman, had no idea that we have, by killing God, drunk "up the sea," wiped "away the entire horizon," "unchained this earth from its sun," and that we may now be "plunging continually" in "empty space," with "night continually closing in on us" (*GS*, 125). Strauss wrongly assumed, like other nineteenth-century thinkers, that even after Darwin, humanity sits on the elevated side of a presumed ontological gap of several spaces between person and plant. In *The Utility and Liability of History for Life*, Nietzsche writes:

Overproud European of the nineteenth century, you are stark raving mad! Your knowledge does not perfect nature, but only kills your own nature. . . . For you, solid ground crumbles away into uncertainty; your life is no longer supported by pillars, but only by spiderwebs that are torn apart by every new grasp of your knowledge. (*ULH*, 9)

Strauss never fully understood that the supports he needed for his own morality were those very ones he claimed to have moved beyond. Although Strauss pays lip service to the death of the traditional Christian conception of God, his constructive proposals require this God.

Nietzsche's own approach to the problem of the death of God is one of utmost seriousness. The profundity of both his analysis and his formulation of how to overcome it arises from the seriousness with which he confronted the problem. The only way to overcome the nihilism that comes with the death of God, Nietzsche thinks, is to face the full ramifications of the "deadly" truth. Nietzsche believes that above all philosophers must be honest. In *Ecce Homo*, he writes, "How much truth does a spirit endure, how much truth does it *dare*? Error (faith in the ideal) is not blindness, error is cowardice" (*EH*, preface, 3). Strauss, for Nietzsche, certainly lacked such courage and honesty. "Strauss demonstrates that he is a hero in words alone and that he shuns every occasion in which he might be required to move from words to grim earnest" (*DS*, 7).[9]

The orbit of Strauss's ethics and "new faith" around an unacknowledged God is not an isolated event in European thought. In fact, Nietzsche finds residues of God in much of the history of Western intellectual thought, even when it takes on a secular guise. Nietzsche is not the first to claim the death of God. Strauss knew—and, in fact, all thinkers from Kant and Hegel onward seem to have known—that the classical concept of God was on shaky ground. They did not, however, seem to display any of the ill affects of the antagonism described by Nietzsche. The reason for this is that, as in Strauss's writings, God's shadow was still projected even in what were thought to be secular values (*GS*, 108). This means that the terrifying consequences of a world of Becoming not grounded by a realm of True Being had not yet honestly been faced. Many of the metaphysical and cosmological presuppositions of theology, Nietzsche observed, were still at work in Europe's "secular" values.[10] When Nietzsche announces God's death, he is thinking about much more than the already disavowed supernatural God of the Bible. The death of God, as Heidegger makes clear, refers not only to the Christian God but to "the suprasensory world in general."[11] God's death means that "the suprasensory world is without effective power. It bestows no life."[12] Nietzsche's announcement about the death of God is far more radical than any made before it.

The Last Man and the Rise of Apathy

Along with the "incomplete nihilism" of David Strauss, Nietzsche also noticed what he called "passive nihilism," which responded to the death of God with a repressive, apathetic, and complacent quietude.

This is the response of the "last man."[13] The last man accepts the futility of human existence that seems to come with the death of God. Michel Haar describes this condition: "Here we have the experience of a will satisfied with meaninglessness, with non-sense, a will happy that there is no longer any sense or any meaning to look for, a will that has found a certain comfort in the absence of meaning."[14]

In the four essays that make up his *Unfashionable Observations*, Nietzsche indicts German culture as vacuous, as containing an opiate that works against "everything subversive and revitalizing" (*RWB*, 3). No one, as Nietzsche looks around, exhibits any taste for life. Rather than face the crisis of the death of God with a desire to grow from it, to take it as the opportunity for positing new values, for finding a new way of affirming life in the world, the modern world has sought relief in the form of various "narcotics." The last man seeks not an active life but a dull security and comfort. When the last man is faced with the great question mark of his existence, he is completely indifferent. "What is love? What is creation? What is longing? What is a star? thus asks the last man, and he blinks" (*Z*, prologue, 5). The last man has no preferences and no worldly desires. He is apathetically neutral. "One no longer becomes poor or rich: both require too much exertion" (*Z*, prologue, 5). The last man is too weary to act and is content merely to bump along, taking the lack of values and apparent meaninglessness of existence as mere fact and fate. The last man takes the problem of *existential nihilism* to be engendered by the very nature of existence. As such, he thinks a life of passive acquiescence and the avoidance of pain, coupled with an occasional smirk of irony, is the most "comfortable" and appropriate response. What else, he thinks, can he do?

Much of what Nietzsche says about the last man can be connected to parts of his discussion in *On the Genealogy of Morals*. In the first essay, Nietzsche states that "we have lost our love of [man], our reverence for him, even the will to him" (*GM*, I:12). What he means is that we now recoil from the idea of a human being that has a sense of strength and a healthy desire for life. We despise the idea of the strong and active human being. Strong individuals, Nietzsche says, have an excess of strength. They are "well born" and feel a sense of nobility (*GM*, I:10). They relish their body, celebrate their health, and enjoy "vigorous, free, joyful activity" (*GM*, I:7). But today, as exemplified in the "last man," there is nothing that "wants to grow greater"

(*GM*, I:12). Rather, things have "become thinner, more good-natured, more prudent, more comfortable, more indifferent, more Chinese, more Christian—there is no doubt that man is getting 'better' all the time" (*GM*, I:12).

In the third essay, Nietzsche's criticism of his contemporary culture as nihilistic is carried out in terms of the fact that it embraces the "ascetic ideal" and amounts to a "will to nothingness." Along with the avoidance of pain by means of various narcotics, humanity represses the despair of nihilism through "mechanical activity" and the pursuit of "petty pleasures." In mechanical activity, one works only so that the mind can be cluttered with meaningless preoccupations. One works only to stay busy, thus leaving little room for any malaise or despair. Mechanical activity is an "absolute regularity, punctilious and unthinking obedience, a mode of life fixed once and for all, fully occupied time, a certain permission, indeed training for 'impersonality,' for self forgetfulness, for '*incuria sui*'" (*GM*, III:18). Accompanying mechanical activity is the pursuit of petty pleasures that are "easily attainable and can be made into a regular event" (*GM*, III:18)—perhaps something like a game of musical chairs with eleven chairs and ten players.

THE LOGIC OF NIHILISM

If indeed there is a disparity between the truth of the nature of reality and the ability to live meaningful lives, then existential nihilism is final and we might as well be "last men." Such a disparity would entail that human life is lived in vain. Insofar as Nietzsche has been the one who has most persuasively argued that we have no right to the belief in the Christian God, he would be the quintessential existential nihilist, the one who has taught us that human life is without meaning. But, in fact, Nietzsche argues passionately and at great length not only that it is possible to create meaning in the godless and purposeless world of Becoming, but also that such a life can be much more than a mere Stoicism or Epicureanism. Nietzsche believes that one can live in the world joyfully and ecstatically. Truth and life can be reconciled; knowledge need not lead to sorrow. The fact that God is dead does not mean that the only possible life is one of repressive and anesthetic comfort. One can live with the deadly truth.

If such a life is possible, then the existential nihilism that follows the death of God and the mood of the last man might itself have an origin, which would mean that it would not be the final word. Existential nihilism might be the result not of an ontological disparity between the "deadly" truth of Becoming and the meaningfulness of human life, but of the fact that we have made a grave mistake in our interpretation of what a meaningful life requires. Existential nihilism would be the result not of reality but merely of a faulty interpretation of reality. Nietzsche writes:

Distress, whether of the soul, body, or intellect, cannot of itself give birth to nihilism (i.e., the radical repudiation of value, meaning, and desirability). Such distress always permits a variety of interpretations. *Rather: it is in one particular interpretation, the Christian-moral one, that nihilism is rooted.* (*WP*, 1; 1885–1886; emphasis added)

He suggests that the feeling of existential nihilism—the despair and apathy accompanying the death of God—is *not* produced merely by the fact that life in the world is radically historical, ephemeral, and transient. The distress, misfortune, and suffering that necessarily arise in such a world do not have to lead to the conclusion that life is without value or meaning. Nietzsche does not take *existential* nihilism to be an ontological problem, rooted in the very nature of existence. Rather, as he goes on to say, the reason we have the problem of existential nihilism, the reason we are unable to affirm our lives in the world as meaningful, valuable, and desirable is because we have *interpreted* distress, misfortune, suffering, and transience in a particular and, for Nietzsche, erroneous way. Nihilism is rooted in the "Christian-moral" interpretation of such phenomena.

At this point, we can begin to see why Nietzsche had two somewhat different attitudes toward Christianity in the modern world. As we have been discussing, he thinks the Christian idea of God is no longer believable. But he also treats the Christian idea with great contempt, arguing that it does great harm to contemporary culture. Although it may seem odd that Nietzsche spends a great deal of time criticizing Christianity when he claims that it is no longer a viable option, these two views are not inconsistent. The death of God results in a conscious sense of nihilism. One feels that life cannot have any meaning. But the reason the death of God leaves a vacuum in which no possibility for a meaningful life appears is because the very values Christianity has given to humanity are already involved in a denigration of worldly existence.

THE CHRISTIAN-MORAL INTERPRETATION

At the heart of the Christian-moral interpretation is the view that distress, suffering, transience, and the like, are in themselves undesirable, things to be avoided, and things thought to be punishments for sin. It is presumed that they are not the conditions of one who is "authentic" or within "ultimate reality." "Everywhere the *will* to misunderstand suffering" gave way to a "reinterpretation of suffering as feelings of guilt, fear, and punishment" (*GM*, III:20). The presence of suffering is taken to be indicative of something in a state of error; it is presumed to be something that must be solved. What these disparaged attitudes have in common is that they all understand distress as militating against the possibility of affirming worldly existence. When Zarathustra encounters such people, he calls them "preachers of death." He complains, "They encounter a sick man or an old man or a corpse, and immediately they say, 'Life is refuted'" (*Z*, I:9). In a later chapter entitled "On Redemption," Zarathustra preaches:

> Because there is suffering in those who will. . . , willing itself and all life were supposed to be—a punishment. And now cloud upon cloud rolled over the spirit, until eventually madness preached, "Everything passes away; therefore everything deserves to pass away." (*Z*, II: 20)

In the Christian-moral interpretation transience, decay, and suffering are presumed to be negative qualities.

Nietzsche agrees that suffering and distress are inextricably linked with life in the world, but he sees the serious ramifications involved in interpreting suffering either as punishment or something ultimately unreal. In *Beyond Good and Evil*, he writes, "You want, if possible—and there is no more insane 'if possible'—*to abolish suffering*" (*BGE*, 225). Only by means of a dishonest lie or bad faith can one remove suffering from the picture of ultimate reality. If distress and suffering are interpreted as things to be avoided, then part and parcel of this interpretation is the notion that activity in the world—or, in short, willing—must be avoided.

> This dominating sense of displeasure is combated, *first,* by means that reduce the feeling of life in general to its lowest point. If possible, will and desire are abolished altogether. . . . [N]o love; no hate; indifference; no revenge; no wealth; no work. (*GM*, III:17)

If suffering is unavoidable and taken to be an indication of something wrong, one should avoid suffering by withdrawing from life in the world.

It is largely because the Christian-moral interpretation of distress leads to this sort of passive and ascetic apathy that Nietzsche distanced himself from Schopenhauer, who, Nietzsche thinks, "is merely the heir of the Christian interpretation" (*TI*, "Skirmishes of an Untimely Man," 21). At the time *The Birth of Tragedy* was written, Nietzsche was greatly under the influence of Schopenhauer's philosophy, convinced by much of its dismal picture of reality. But he did not, even in this early writing, agree with Schopenhauer's pessimistic conclusion concerning the actual value of existence. For Schopenhauer, existence amounted to nothing more than a ceaseless struggle with suffering. Furthermore, struggle and suffering are, according to Schopenhauer, only increased with every effort of the will to abate them. In Schopenhauer's words:

> No attained object of desire can give lasting satisfaction, but merely a fleeting gratification. . . . Therefore, so long as our consciousness is filled by our will, so long as we are given up to the throng of desires with their constant hopes and fears, so long as we are the subject of willing, we can never have lasting happiness nor peace.[15]

Unable to escape the suffering caused by willing, Schopenhauer recommended a life of asceticism.

Nietzsche certainly accepted Schopenhauer's claims concerning the ubiquity of suffering, but he did not accept the need to withdraw from the world. In many ways, as Richard Schacht points out, *The Birth of Tragedy* is to be "regarded as an attempt to meet this challenge, and to establish a viable alternative verdict."[16] The task of *The Birth of Tragedy* is to find a way to affirm one's existence *within* such a reality, while recognizing the "pessimistic" truth about reality and its inclusion of pain and suffering as unavoidable qualities.

Without this sort of affirmation of worldly life, the world and human existence can be understood only nihilistically. In his "Attempt at a Self-Criticism," a preface added to a second edition of *The Birth of Tragedy*, Nietzsche gives a brief account of the judgment of life that he finds necessarily contained in the Christian-moral interpretation.

> For in the face of morality (particularly Christian, unconditional morality), life *must* constantly and inevitably be in the wrong, because life is

something essentially amoral—in the end, crushed beneath the weight of contempt and eternal denial, life *must* be felt to be undesirable, valueless in itself. (*BT,* "Attempt at a Self-Criticism," 5)

In the Christian-moral interpretation, something "moral" is something with no distress or suffering. Because the world of Becoming is amoral in the sense that suffering and distress are a necessary part of existence, excusing neither the good nor the unjust from its embrace, the Christian-moral interpretation—which takes suffering to be a sign of something in the wrong—must see this world to be at fault.

What Nietzsche is suggesting is that the ubiquitous feeling of futility that follows the death of God is caused by an initial attempt to *justify* human existence in the world. If existence strikes one as in need of external justification, then it is implied that existence is not justified in itself, that something is already presumed to be wrong with it. This means that the conscious nihilism brought on by the death of God is caused by a *prior* nihilism or denigration of worldly life. Alan White, who captures this thought well, says:

> I therefore suggest that the first step towards nihilism . . . is the step taken with the judgment that the existence of our world of becoming would be justified only through a *purpose* that it has not yet reached, through an "infinitely valuable" unity that underlies it, or through its relation to another world, a "true world" of being. This step, like the step to rejection, is a negation in that it contains, at least implicitly, the judgment that our "world of becoming" as it presents itself, *in isolation* from such purpose, unity, or truth, "ought not to exist."[17]

Put another way, European culture is faced with the *explicit* and conscious belief in the valuelessness of the world that accompanies the death of God because in the very values and interpretations previously given to the world is already an *implicit* denigration of the value of life in this world. "It is my contention that all the values by which mankind now sums up its supreme desiderata are *decadence-values*" (*A,* 6). For Nietzsche, decadence refers to a decline in the ability to live in the world on the world's terms. Nietzsche associates decadence with a weak will and intolerance for distress and turmoil. To be decadent is to be unable to accept the world of Becoming as reality. Decadent values are those that accept this judgment.

Nietzsche notices that this decadence has led to the hope that this world of Becoming and distress may not be the "True World," that maybe, above and beyond this world, there exists a "True World" where such things do not occur.

> Any distinction between a "true" and an "apparent" world—whether in the Christian manner or in the manner of Kant (in the end, an underhanded Christian)—is only a suggestion of decadence, a symptom of the *decline of life*. (*TI*, "'Reason' in Philosophy," 6)

Furthermore, Nietzsche notices that this decadence is a form of nihilism: "To invent fables about a world 'other' than this one has no meaning at all, unless an instinct of slander, detraction, and suspicion against life has gained the upper hand in us" (*TI*, "'Reason' in Philosophy," 6).

The subtitle to Nietzsche's chapter "How the 'True World' Finally Became a Fable" in the *Twilight of the Idols* is "The History of an Error." The error is the equation of truth and meaning with static Being, with that which is without any sort of change. This equation is the defining characteristic of the history of the West and its intellectual interpretations of the world.

> You asked me which of the philosophers' traits are really idiosyncrasies? For example, their lack of historical sense, their hatred of the very idea of becoming, their Egypticism. They think that they show their respect for something when they de-historicize it, *sub specie aeterni*. . . . Death, change, old age, as well as procreation and growth, are to their minds objections—even refutations. Whatever has being does not become; whatever becomes does not have being. Now they all believe, desperately even, in what has being. (*TI*, "'Reason' in Philosophy," 1)

The true things of value, these philosophers claim, "cannot be derived from this transitory, seductive, deceptive, paltry world, from this turmoil of delusion and lust. Rather from the lap of Being, the intransitory, the hidden god, the 'thing-in-itself'—there must be their basis, and nowhere else" (*BGE*, 2). It is from this basic presupposition concerning the equation of meaning with static Being that the pejorative view of suffering and distress stems. Perfection and becoming are thought to be antithetical to one another (*HATH*, I:145). The reason that the conscious nihilism of the late nineteenth century is the outcome of this error is that when the "True World of Being" is discovered to be a fable, we are left with no immediate way to find meaning and value in a world that lacks the qualities of the "True World of Being."

Conscious nihilism, we can now say, is the result of a series of hierarchical dualisms[18] in which one component of a conceptual pair is thought to have ontological priority. By this, I mean that in the traditional antinomies or binary oppositions of, for example, being/becoming, good/evil, truth/appearance, permanence/change, mind/body, pleasure/pain, and beauty/ugliness, the first concept, usually referred to as "positive," is thought to be prior, more original, and capable of existing in its own right. The positive and negative concepts are thought to be directly opposed to one another and capable of segregation. In this hierarchical conceptual scheme, one can have, it is thought, being without becoming, good without evil, mind without body, permanence without change, and so on. But, for Nietzsche, the "positive" concepts cannot exist without the "negative" ones. The relationship is not hierarchical but interdependent. They are thoroughly interrelated. For Nietzsche, as Stanley Rosen writes, Heraclitus was correct and Parmenides incorrect.[19] The Christian-moral interpretation of distress presupposes this hierarchically dualistic logic.

To those who wish to eradicate the negative qualities from their life or from what is thought to constitute ultimate reality, Nietzsche states, "How little you know of human *happiness*, you comfortable people, for happiness and unhappiness are sisters and even twins" (*GS*, 338). And again, in *Beyond Good and Evil*, Nietzsche writes:

> It might even be possible that what constitutes the value of these good and revered things is precisely that they are insidiously related, tied to, and involved with these wicked, seemingly opposite things—maybe even one with them in essence. Maybe! (*BGE*, 2)[20]

The components of these conceptual pairs, for Nietzsche, are not opposed to one another. They are, as Alexander Nehamas writes, "points along a single continuum."[21]

The despair caused by God's death is itself caused by the values contained within Christianity—namely, the presumed ontological priority of the "categories of Being." This is the reason that Nietzsche is not content merely to report the death of God. He must turn his attention to Christianity and its latent denial of the meaning of human life in the world. In sum, the values of Christianity make it impossible for human beings to affirm life in the world.

NOTES

1. Because *The Will to Power* is a collection of unpublished notes, unscrupulously edited by Nietzsche's sister, it is a controversial source for Nietzsche's philosophy. This presents a problem for trying to understand a good number of Nietzsche's key concepts. My primary use of *The Will to Power* will be to draw passages that can be used to orient and shape a discussion that will take us through the published writings. Proceeding in this way should greatly reduce the importance of the problem of how *The Will to Power* is to be used. So that passages from *The Will to Power* can be put into a larger context, I include the date of each note in the citation.

2. For a discussion that lists and attempts to sort out these different uses, see Alan White, "Nietzschean Nihilism: A Typology," *International Studies in Philosophy* 19 (Summer 1987): 29–44.

3. Morgan, *What Nietzsche Means*, 4.

4. This thesis is sustained by Walter Kaufmann, who writes, "To escape nihilism . . . is Nietzsche's greatest and most persistent problem" (*Nietzsche: Philosopher, Psychologist, Antichrist*, 101). Michael Allen Gillespie, relying on the fact that the term *nihilism* does not appear in Nietzsche's published work until 1886, argues that nihilism is *not* the central question of Nietzsche's thought (*Nihilism before Nietzsche* [Chicago: University of Chicago Press, 1995], 178). However, Nietzsche's concern with nihilism should not be limited only to the times the word *nihilism* occurs. For example, *The Birth of Tragedy*, the earliest of Nietzsche's writings, is very much concerned with the question of how one is to "justify existence." This question points to the centrality of the problem, albeit not by name, of nihilism.

5. David Harvey writes, "There is abundant evidence to suggest that most 'modern' writers have recognized that the only secure thing about modernity is its insecurity, its penchant, even, for 'totalizing chaos'" (*The Condition of Postmodernity: An Enquiry into the Origins of Cultural Change* [Oxford: Blackwell, 1990], 11).

6. Milan Kundera's novel *The Unbearable Lightness of Being*, trans. Michael Henry Heim (New York: Harper & Row, 1984), can be read as a Nietzschean meditation on the contrast between a life of "lightness," in which nothing acquires permanent significance because events dissolve as they occur, and one lived with an "unbearable responsibility" and profound heaviness, in which all events are forever recurring.

7. David Michael Levin, "Psychopathology in the Epoch of Nihilism," in *Pathologies of the Modern Self: Postmodern Studies on Narcissism, Schizophrenia, and Depression,* ed. David Michael Levin (New York: New York University Press, 1987), 41.

8. Nietzsche takes this title from a verse of Byron's *Manfred*, which he quotes: "Sorrow is knowledge: they who know the most/ Must mourn the deepest o'er the fatal truth: / The tree of knowledge is not that of life."

9. The one philosopher whose courage and truthfulness made him admirable in Nietzsche's eyes was Schopenhauer. In fact, the tribute to him in *Schopenhauer as Educator* is largely in honor of Schopenhauer the man, not his philosophy.

10. For a discussion substantiating Nietzsche's claims regarding the secularization of theological ideas and ways of thinking in Romantic literature, see M. H. Abrams, *Natural Supernaturalism: Tradition and Revolution in Romantic Literature* (New York: Norton, 1971).

11. Martin Heidegger, "The Word of Nietzsche: 'God Is Dead,'" in *The Question Concerning Technology and Other Essays,* trans. William Lovitt (New York: Harper & Row, 1977), 61.

12. Heidegger, "The Word of Nietzsche," 61.

13. For a critique of our own late twentieth-century American culture as that of the "last man," see Allan Bloom, *The Closing of the American Mind* (New York: Simon & Schuster, 1987), 78 and 141–240.

14. Michel Haar, *Nietzsche and Metaphysics*, trans. and ed. Michael Gendre (Albany: State University of New York Press, 1996), 11.

15. Arthur Schopenhauer, *The World as Will and Idea,* vol. 1, trans. R. B. Haldane and J. Kemp (London: Routledge & Kegan Paul, 1957), 253–54.

16. Richard Schacht, *Nietzsche* (London: Routledge, 1983), 478.

17. Alan White, "Nietzschean Nihilism," 30.

18. The term *hierarchical dualism* is taken from Bernd Magnus, *Nietzsche's Existential Imperative* (Bloomington: Indiana University Press, 1978), 180.

19. Stanley Rosen, *The Mask of Enlightenment: Nietzsche's Zarathustra* (Cambridge: Cambridge University Press, 1995), 56.

20. In *The Will to Power*, Nietzsche writes, "Health and sickness are not essentially different, as the ancient physicians and some practitioners even today suppose. One must not make of them distinct principles or entities that fight over the living organism and turn it into their arena" (*WP*, 47; 1888).

21. Alexander Nehamas, *Nietzsche: Life as Literature* (Cambridge, Mass.: Harvard University Press, 1985), 44.

3

The Rise and Development of the Christian-Moral Interpretation, Part 1

Socratic Platonism

In the previous chapter, I mentioned that much of Nietzsche's criticism of Christianity revolves around the fact that Christianity privileges the "positive" concepts of static Being. In doing so, it presupposes that anything qualified by the "negative" qualities of Becoming is inferior. Because human life in the world is inextricably bound up with the categories of Becoming, the meaning of human life in the world is denigrated. In this chapter, I would like to continue my discussion of the Christian-moral interpretation, paying special attention to its history. My purpose is to discuss, in more detail, the problems Nietzsche finds with a value system and worldview that privileges the categories of static Being. In this chapter and the next, I discuss three episodes in the history of Western intellectual history that Nietzsche associates with this value system: Socratic-Platonism, Christianity, and Kantian philosophy. After some introductory comments, in this chapter, I examine the role Socratic-Platonism plays in this history.

The Christian-moral interpretation of distress should be understood as an example of what Nietzsche calls "improvement-morality." An improvement morality is a system of practices that seeks both to improve what it takes to be a faulty human condition indigenous to life in the world and to eradicate the problems plaguing human life in the world, such as pain, suffering, evil, and distress. It is a morality that attempts to remove the "negative qualities." Although this may seem optimistic, Nietzsche insists that it results in making the situation worse because such an improvement is based on a misunderstanding of the nature of

reality. The "negative" qualities of existence cannot simply be removed, nor are they simply undesirable. An "improvement-morality"
can result only in a sort of *maquillage* and, as such, the ability to affirm the world as it is is seriously threatened through this repression. It
can succeed, as we will see, only by turning humanity's attention away
from the world, the body, the passions, the instincts, a life of eros, a
feeling of strength, and a strong sense of self.

Nietzsche's strong rhetoric against the possibility of "improving"
the human situation leads, quite quickly, to a possible misinterpreta-
tion. It may seem that he is suggesting that human beings are perfectly formed in their natural state, so that the problem of the human
situation is caused *only* by accretive doctrines, social customs, and
other such "unnatural" layers. To be sure, this is an aspect of his position. In one respect, Nietzsche celebrates the death of God because
it inaugurates the project of remaking ourselves and shedding a self
that was cultivated on decadent values. "When will all these shadows
of God cease to darken our minds? When will we complete our de-
deification of nature? When may we begin to "naturalize" humanity
in terms of a pure, newly discovered, newly redeemed nature?" (*GS*,
109). However, a dedeified and renaturalized human being is not a
static entity, already perfectly formed. "There are no eternally enduring substances; matter is as much of an error as the God of the Eleat-
ics" (*GS*, 109). Reality is not composed of static substances of Being
but is rather Becoming. The world is, Nietzsche writes, "will to power
and nothing else" (*BGE*, 36). One of the things that Nietzsche surely
intended by this remark is that all things *will to overcome themselves*.
The secret imparted to Zarathustra by life is "I am *that which must
always overcome itself*. Indeed, you call it a will to procreate or a
drive to an end, to something higher, farther, more manifold: but all
this is one, and one secret" (*Z*, II:12). Reality is composed of entities
that are involved in a constant struggle with themselves and others.
Here we find Nietzsche articulating a certain need for improvement
in the human situation. Zarathustra teaches not the *Mensch* but the
Übermensch. "*I teach you the overman*. Man is something that shall
be overcome" (*Z*, prologue, 3). Zarathustra characterizes the human
situation with the following image: "Man is a rope, tied between
beast and overman—a rope over an abyss. A dangerous across, a
dangerous on-the-way, a dangerous looking-back, a dangerous
shuddering and stopping" (*Z*, prologue, 3). This passage makes note

of a crucial point in Nietzsche's understanding of humanity. That which is overcome is not only the unnatural and nihilistic self created by a culture of decadence but also the "beast." Unlike John Locke, who assumed that the natural self-preservative instincts of the human being followed a natural law, thereby something resembling a divinely sanctioned morality, Nietzsche did not assume such a pacific return to nature. Thus, for Nietzsche, humanity must strive to overcome its natural, "beastly" state. Humanity must, in a sense, "improve." It must move beyond the "human, all too human."

What is it about "improvement-morality," then, that Nietzsche rejects? The type of "improvement" to which he is opposed is that which merely attempts to eradicate the sources of distress by removing the "negative" concepts from ultimate reality. If one merely proceeds to ameliorate the situation by exorcising the brutish forces, the result is a sort of lobotomy. In this case, "improvement" signifies the "same thing as 'tamed,' 'weakened,' 'discouraged,' 'made refined,' 'made effete,' 'emasculated' (thus almost the same thing as *harmed*)" (*GM*, III:21). Nietzsche's program of overcoming is not a stance invoking the need for this sort of improvement. "The last thing *I* should promise would be to 'improve' mankind" (*EH*, preface, 2). Nietzsche, it can be said, seeks to overcome the human situation by means of *expansion* and acceptance, while the various "improvement-moralities" hope to improve the human situation by *subtraction* and denial. Improvement-morality "has at all times laid the stress of discipline on extirpation" (*TI*, "Morality as Anti-Nature," 1). Nietzsche makes this clear when he writes that "all the old moral monsters are agreed on this: *il faut tuer les passions*" (*TI*, "Morality as Anti-Nature," 1). He also draws attention to the Sermon on the Mount and its absurd call to pluck out eyes that give rise to sexual passions. For Nietzsche, "overcoming" means becoming more natural by acting and, indeed, flourishing as a human being. The various "improvement-moralities" deny that the essence of the human being is rooted in the world, the flesh, and the instincts. Rather, they seek the essence of a human being in some realm of "pure spirit." They purport that something is flawed in the bodily constitution of a human being and its life in the world; something is in error. Nietzsche's program of overcoming does not carry with it the idea that the human being as such is in error, only that it is possible to achieve and expand into a greater quality of life.

To make these differences a little clearer, it is helpful to say more about what Nietzsche means by "morality." When he writes that "every naturalism in morality—that is, *every healthy morality*—is dominated by an instinct of life" (*TI*, "Morality as Anti-Nature," 4; emphasis added), it is clear that he is not opposed to morality outright, notwithstanding the fact that Nietzsche's own language often seems to suggest this opposition. He is not, in other words, suggesting that human beings refrain from cultivating themselves on certain ideals. In fact, good portions of Nietzsche's writings are concerned with the idea of achieving human excellence.[1] Nietzsche's opposition to morality has its eyes on those ideals that are hostile to the "instincts of life." Nietzsche's program of self-overcoming is not involved in the attempt to remove bodily instincts, but at sublimating these desires into higher, but still worldly, purposes.

By attempting to remove the "negative" aspects of human existence, improvement-morality removes the very things human beings need to flourish. Flourishing, expanding, and "overcoming" require contradictions, tensions, and suffering. "Well-constituted, joyful mortals who are far from regarding their unstable equilibrium between 'animal and angel' as necessarily an argument against existence. . . . It is precisely such 'contradictions' that seduce one to existence" (*GM*, III:2). For Nietzsche, to seduce into existence means that one is drawn into immersion in the world of Becoming.

We can get a still better understanding of Nietzsche's opposition to improvement-morality and Christianity by introducing the final sentence of the last of Nietzsche's writings, *Ecce Homo*: "Have I been understood?—*Dionysus versus the Crucified*" (*EH*, "Why I Am a Destiny," 9). It is not unfair to take this line as the final summation of Nietzsche's philosophy. Represented by the tragic figure of Dionysus, Nietzsche's philosophy is to be understood in opposition to Christianity, as a contrasting and opposing alternative worldview and way of life. Dionysus represents the tragic philosophy and worldview of Greek culture prior to the time of Euripides and Socrates. The Crucified represents the optimistic improvement morality of Christianity.

There are some interesting parallels between the figures of Dionysus and the Crucified. Both are sons of a god, and each is born of a mortal woman. Dionysus is divine because after his premature birth from Semele, he is sewn into the thigh of Zeus, his father, and born again. Common to each is a life of persecution by forces that felt threatened by their respective religious messages. In turn, Dionysus and Christ suffer excruciatingly painful deaths. Christ is executed on the cross; Dionysus is torn to pieces and devoured by the Titans.

Nietzsche claims that the major point of contrast between these two figures resides in the attitude toward suffering that each embody. Both affirm that suffering is a part of human life in the world. But in these affirmations are different attitudes toward suffering. In the case of the Crucified, suffering "counts as an objection to this life, as a formula for its condemnation." Suffering is accepted only as "the path to a holy existence" (*WP*, 1052; 1888). But, in the case of Dionysus, "being is counted as *holy enough* to justify even a monstrous amount of suffering" (*WP*, 1052; 1888). For the Crucified, suffering carries with it an objection to life because the categories of Being are given ontological priority. Thus, one forsakes the realm of Becoming, seeking meaning in another realm. For Dionysus, there is, Nietzsche states, "an affirmation of life, life whole and not denied or in part" (*WP*, 1052; 1888). There is no yearning for an improved life elsewhere. One way of understanding Nietzsche's entire philosophical output is to see it as an attempt to understand how and why the tragic but affirmative worldview represented by Dionysus has been replaced by the Christian view. The triumph of the Christian view over the tragic Dionysian view is of great concern for Nietzsche. The ultimate outcome of the Christian worldview is the apathetic, passionless, and indifferent "last man."

SOCRATES

And behold: Apollo could not live without Dionysus!

—*Nietzsche,* The Birth of Tragedy

I have given to understand how it was that Socrates fascinated: he seemed to be a physician, a savior.

—*Nietzsche,* The Twilight of the Idols

While Nietzsche chooses to call the primary target of his genealogy of modern nihilism the "Christian-moral" interpretation of distress, he does not take Christianity to be the original, positing fountain of the "highest," but nihilistic, values. Rather, Christianity is an outgrowth and development of an earlier decadent nihilist: Socrates.[2] When Nietzsche examines the life and work of Socrates, he discovers that Socrates was decadent, pronouncing life to be no good. In *The Gay Science*, Nietzsche interprets Socrates' dying words, "O Crito, I owe Asclepius a rooster," to mean "for those who have ears: 'O Crito, life is a disease'." Socrates, the passage continues, "*suffered* life" (*GS*, 340). Nietzsche is referring to the tradition of giving Asclepius a sacrificial gift after being healed of various ailments. By offering Asclepius a rooster, Socrates, Nietzsche suggests, is claiming that his death is really healing him of what ails him, namely life itself. In *The Twilight of the Idols*, Nietzsche credits himself with having recognized "Socrates and Plato to be symptoms of degeneration, tools of the Greek dissolution, pseudo-Greek, anti-Greek" (*TI*, "The Problem of Socrates," 2).

The Quest for Apollo

What was it about life in the world that caused Socrates to suffer from it? What presented him with a problem? Why does he yearn for death?[3] Nietzsche sees in Socrates someone unable to accept the tragic reality of living in a world of Becoming, with its deadly truth. But Socrates—and this is the real problem for Nietzsche—did not merely suffer passively, did not merely suffer this physiological dissatisfaction as his fate. Had he, he would not be Nietzsche's bête noire. Rather, Socrates found it necessary to interpret his distress in a particular way because he could neither affirm the world of Becoming nor accept a fate of discontent. He needed to convince himself that his unpleasant and unsatisfactory existence in the world was not his ultimate fate or the experience of one in touch with ultimate reality.

In *The Birth of Tragedy*, Nietzsche describes what he takes to be two fundamental descriptive principles: Apollo and Dionysus. They are usually used to describe types of art but are also applicable in a more general sense. Named after the god of the sun, the Apollonian principle refers to that which is pleasant and dreamlike. It presents images, exemplified in the visual arts, that are pleasant, proportional, orderly, and unambiguous. It is the *principium individuationis*, creating form out of chaos (*BT*, 1). Apollonian images are static and have a sense of order. In contrast, Dionysian art, named after the god who brought wine to the Greeks, is characterized by intoxication, spontaneity, and disorder. It is immersed in the "flux of things,"[4] thereby breaking "the spell of individuation" (*BT*, 1). It is best characterized by music.

Although Nietzsche sometimes described these two principles as equal to one another, it is clear that the Dionysian principle represents a more truthful account of reality. Dionysian art speaks with a "true voice," while the Apollonian speaks with "lies" (*BT*, 16). For Nietzsche reality is Dionysian, which means that at its core, reality is chaotic. For this reason, reality seems quite terrifying, Nietzsche thinks, insofar as it presents a constant threat to our sense of individual identity, giving way to a feeling of helplessness. The Dionysian man resembles Hamlet: "Both have once looked truly into the essence of things, they have *gained knowledge*, and nausea inhibits action" (*BT*, 7).

Socrates wanted to show that ultimate reality is not Dionysian, that it is not an ambiguous, disorderly muddle. Socrates was, Nietzsche states again and again, "optimistic" about the possibility of "improving" the human situation and making reality straighter, less ambiguous, less threatening, and more tolerable. He wanted to make it, in Nietzsche's terms, more "Apollonian"—more orderly, rational, and comprehensible. Socrates suggested that the world of Becoming, with its change, decay, deception, and lack of stability, is merely an illusion of something perfect, an imperfect copy or "particular" of a perfect, unchanging "form."

In Plato's famous allegory of the cave, we find Socrates describing what he takes to be the human existential situation. The physical world is described as a cave, and Socrates quickly adds the pejorative gloss that the cave is a "prison."[5] Human beings are locked down, "with their necks and legs in fetters."[6] What is known to be reality is taken from observing shadows on the wall of the cave. Because the prisoners are locked down and cannot turn their necks, they do not know that the shadows are merely images, poor ones at that, of a greater reality. The human condition in the world, for Socrates, is one of ignorance. What we see and experience in the world is not the True World; it is only an apparent world.

The way to escape the prison of illusions is to acquire what Socrates calls a "philosophical nature."

We must accept as agreed this trait of the philosophical nature, that it is ever enamored of the kind of knowledge which reveals to [the philosophers] *something of that essence which is eternal, and is not wandering between the two poles of generation and decay.*[7]

Therefore, the True World is eternal, static, stable, and unchanging, while falsehood is that which has a history, changes, and decays. Those who have the "philosophical nature" must have, Socrates continues, "the spirit of truthfulness, reluctance to admit falsehood in any form, the hatred of it and the love of truth."[8] In other words, they must love the eternally unchanging and hate the decaying and changing.

Socrates thought the problematic nature of life in the cave could be escaped through "reason." "Rationality was then hit upon as the savior" (*TI*, "The Problem of Socrates," 10). Through reason one could discern a realm of truths that is absolute, universal, and not subject to the ever-changing, never stable, erosive nature of the apparent world of Becoming. If one can discern such truths, they can be used as a basis for action, which could then "improve" the human condition, allowing one to escape the trouble of this world. Nietzsche writes:

> There is . . . a profound *illusion* that first saw the light of the world in the person of Socrates: the unshakable faith that thought, using the thread of causality, can penetrate the deepest abysses of being, and that thought is capable not only of knowing being but even of *correcting* it. (*BT*, 15)

Socrates thought that reason could show that below or above the Dionysian world of change is something stable, static, eternal, and unchanging. It could straighten things out and be used to construct a metaphysics that would show the ambiguous and Dionysian elements to be less than real. Socrates' mission, which now stands as "the emblem . . . above the gates of science," is "to make existence appear comprehensible and thus justified" (*BT*, 15). The Socratic faith in reason is a "turning point" and the "vortex of world-history" (*BT*, 15). Socrates is, Nietzsche writes:

> the prototype of the theoretical optimist who, with his faith that the nature of things can be fathomed, ascribes to knowledge and insight the power of a panacea, while understanding error as the evil *par excellence*. To fathom the depths and to separate true knowledge from appearance and error, seemed to Socratic man the noblest, even the only truly human vocation. (*BT*, 15)

It surely seems odd to call Socrates—with his optimism that there is a meaning to all this chaos—a decadent nihilist. But Nietzsche finds this faith in Socratic reason to be a sign, not of progress, but of a newly emerging inability to ascribe, with confidence, an intraworldly meaning to human existence. Nietzsche is suspicious of the Socratic conception of reason and the uses to which it is put. "I seek," he writes, "to comprehend what idiosyncrasy begot that Socratic equation of reason, virtue, and happiness: that most bizarre of all equations, which, moreover, is opposed to all the instincts of the earlier Greeks" (*TI*, "The Problem of Socrates," 4). And, being opposed to those tragic but affirmative Greeks, Nietzsche regards this particular need to make reality intelligible and systematic as a sign of degeneration, which will ultimately lead to otherworldliness, and the position that life in the world cannot be affirmed as it is.

"With Socrates, Greek taste changes in favor of dialectics" (*TI*, "The Problem of Socrates," 5). Nietzsche argues that in the Greek culture prior to Socrates there was no need to explicate and prove the meaning of the world by means of dialectic. To the aristocrats of this culture, the meaning and value of this world was not in question. The world was not in need of "justification." The need to go below or above the surface, in this case, betrays a certain dissatisfaction with what one is faced with. These early Greeks, not being decadent, could remain in the world. They knew, as Nietzsche knows, "that honest things, like honest men, do not carry their reasons in their hands," so that "what must first be proved is worth little" (*TI*, "The Problem of Socrates," 5).

Nietzsche asks, rhetorically, if the "modesty and cheerfulness of theoretical man—could not that very Socratism be a symptom of decline, fatigue, infection, and the anarchical dissolution of the instincts?" (*BT*, "Attempt at a Self-Criticism," 1). Nietzsche the genealogist wants to know what "all of science [*Wissenschaft*] means as a symptom of life?" "Might the scientific approach be nothing but fear, flight from pessimism? A subtle form of self-defense against—*the truth?*" (*BT*, "Attempt at a Self-Criticism, 1.*) The truth to which Nietzsche is referring is the "deadly" truth of Dionysian reality. Socratic-theoretical science is a defense against the truth insofar as it is, Nietzsche thinks, merely a device used optimistically, but superficially, to argue that this Dionysian world of Becoming is not the True World. In a passage from *The Gay Science* entitled "The teachers of the purpose of existence," Nietzsche notes how this sort of reason can lead to otherworldliness.

> From time to time this instinct, which is at work equally in the highest and the basest men—the instinct for the preservation of the species—

erupts as reason and as passion of the spirit. Then it is surrounded by a resplendent retinue of reasons and tries with all the force at its command to make us forget that at bottom it is instinct, drive, folly, lack of reasons. Life *shall* be loved, *because*—! Man *shall* advance himself and his neighbor, *because*—! What names all these Shalls and Becauses receive in the future! In order that what happens necessarily and always, spontaneously and without any purpose may henceforth appear to be done for some purpose and strike men as rational and an ultimate commandment, the ethical teacher comes on stage, as the teacher of the purpose of existence; and to this end he invents a second, different existence and unhinges by means of his new mechanics the old, ordinary existence. (*GS*, 1)

This need to justify, to explain, and interpret the world with "becauses" signals a growing dissatisfaction with the world as it is. The Socratic project of reason betrays a dissatisfaction with the world of Becoming and a lack of confidence that a human life in the world of Becoming can be meaningful in itself.

Nietzsche's critique of Socratic reason is tricky and needs to be put in the more balanced, nuanced environment of his greater thought. It is crucial to understand just what Nietzsche opposes in Socrates' "faith in reason." First of all, Nietzsche is not opposed to reason in a generic sense. Nor is he denying that human beings have a certain capacity to reason. There are plenty of places in Nietzsche's writings where he both advocates the use of reason and criticizes others for being unreasonable.

What Nietzsche objects to in Socrates' understanding of reason is the view that something is reasonable, logical, and true only when it admits no change, no transition, and no decay. For Socrates, the rational must be something simple; the truthful has pure self-identity. This is why Socrates argues that the philosopher should love only that which does not wander between the "two poles of generation and decay." For our purposes, it is helpful to call the sort of reason Nietzsche opposes "ahistorical reason." I will also use the adjective *ahistorical* to refer to the conceptions of truth and logic Nietzsche opposed.

What occurs in the Socratic allegiance to ahistorical reason is that truth comes to be understood as something utterly and purely objective in the sense that it betrays no trace of "subjectivity." For Nietzsche, the subjectivity of thinking is unavoidable; thought is perspectival and sensuous. Philosophical thought has attempted to cloak these facts. Concerning the prejudices of philosophers, Nietzsche writes:

What provokes one to look at all philosophers half suspiciously, half mockingly is . . . that they are not honest enough in their work, although they all make a lot of virtuous noise when the problem of truthfulness is touched even remotely. They all pose as if they had discovered and reached their real opinions through the self-development of a cold, pure, divinely unconcerned dialectic . . . while at bottom it as an assumption, a hunch, indeed a kind of "inspiration"—most often a desire of the heart that has been filtered and made abstract—that they defend with reasons they have sought after the fact. (*BGE*, 5)

In the *Phaedo*—Nietzsche's primary text for explicating the meaning of Socratic reason—Socrates tells Simmias, "We are in fact convinced that if we are ever to have pure knowledge of anything, we must get rid of the body and contemplate things by themselves with the soul itself."[9] When the soul "investigates by itself," Socrates says a little later, "it passes into the realm of the pure and everlasting and immortal and changeless."[10] Socratic reason is entirely disembodied.

Nietzsche, as Manfred Riedel writes, does not want to sacrifice the notion of reason, but "on the contrary, Nietzsche expands and deepens this concept by adding a dimension which had become further and further removed from metaphysics in the course of its history."[11] He wants to make reason, in a sense, more "earthy," more capable of understanding and maintaining the complexity of reality without simplifying it. Nietzsche wants to take up, with earnest seriousness, the one question that philosophy has always been faced with:

How can something arise from its opposite, for example something rational from something irrational, something sentient from something dead, logic from illogic, disinterested contemplation from willful desire, living for others from egoism, truth from error? (*HATH*, I:1)

Nietzsche, as we have seen, begins with the presupposition that opposing concepts are interdependent and that reality is complex enough to support both concepts. If this is true, the conception of reason must somehow be expanded to account for such complexities. Socratic ahistorical reason cannot account for this complexity, and it deals with this puzzle by denying that such a thing can occur.

Metaphysical philosophy has up to now helped itself get past this difficulty by denying that one emerged from the other and assuming that more highly valued things had a miraculous origin, immediately out of the core and essence of the "thing in itself." (*HATH*, I:1)[12]

The Socratic faith in reason is the epitome of the philosopher's idio-syncratic "lack of historical sense" (*TI*, "'Reason' in Philosophy," 1). Unable to tolerate, let alone live with, the idea that the world and hu-manity display a depth and complexity greatly outstretching the bounds of a very simple logic, Socrates found it necessary to deny that such apostasies could be True. The True is rather the simple, static, unambiguous, and eternal. The philosopher urges us to attribute "no truth to anything which it views indirectly as being subject to varia-tion."[13] Truth and corporeality are directly opposed. Reality must be Apollonian, not Dionysian.

In some ways, Socrates masculinizes the concept of truth. Women, for Socrates, are completely unsuited for the pursuit of truth. They are far too emotional, bodily, unstable, and passionate. In fact, they ex-emplify those qualities that are directly opposed to the qualities of ahistorical truth. When his death is imminent, Socrates chastises his friends for weeping.

> Really, my friends, what a way to behave! Why, that was my main rea-son for sending away the women, to prevent this sort of disturbances, because I am told that one should make one's end in a tranquil frame of mind. Calm yourself and try to be brave.[14]

For Socrates, truth is unlike a woman; it is clear, without passion, without sensuality, and certainly without a body. It is concerned with Forms, not particulars.

In contrast to Socrates' understanding of truth, Nietzsche asks, "Supposing truth were a woman—what then?" (*BGE*, preface). Sup-pose, it might be added, that truth is neither static nor disembodied? If truth is regendered as bodily, sensual, emotional, and artistic, in short, as a woman, perhaps then the world, with its desires, bodies, transitions, "negative" qualities, and vicissitudes, might be true. It might, in other words, be meaningful.[15] Truth, Nietzsche often says, is bloody. It is in this respect, I suggest, that we understand Nietzsche's frequently quoted statements in which he denies the existence of truth. The truth that does not exist is the pure, unadulterated, and un-tainted Truth sought by Socrates. The general bias of Western thought is that Truth and appearance are opposed to one another, as are Truth and variation. Nietzsche's criticisms of truth, reason, and the True World of Being are not denials of truth, reason, and the possibility that there is a true way in which the world really is. Richard Schacht is correct when he writes that what Nietzsche is denying is "that there is no world or reality or realm that *transcends* that in which we live, and with reference to which *this* world is unreal, illusory, a mere appearance, or merely phenomenal."[16]

For Nietzsche, reality cannot be fathomed by Socrates' understanding of ahistorical reason. Woman, Nietzsche says, has "not allowed herself to be won by the dogmatist" (*BGE*, preface). Lurking at the base of this particular suspicion is Nietzsche's view of the relationship between language and reality. In the posthumously published work *Truth and Lie in an Extra-Moral Sense*, Nietzsche asks, "Is language the adequate expression of all realities" (*TL*, 45)? He answers no; the fit between words and the things of the world is not, by any means, tight. Language is "awkward" (*BGE*, 24). When taken literally, language presents a world composed of static and isolated entities. But if the world is characterized by Becoming, language, at least in its predominant grammatical structure, can get to reality only metaphorically. Linguistic expressions of the nature of reality do not and cannot exhaust the meaning of that which they attempt to describe.

The danger of the Socratic understanding of reason is that it purports an ability to explain events and entities with a dogmatic certainty. The use of ahistorical reason, as it originates in Socrates and culminates in modern science, denies the metaphorical relationship between language and reality. Ahistorical reason cloaks the diversity and fluidity of reality. It simplifies reality. Nietzsche is not suggesting that one abandon the project of reason, but he is pointing to the reductionistic tendencies of Socratic reason. In the hands of Socrates, language goes from being a metaphor to being a "concept." In her book *Nietzsche and Metaphor*, Sarah Kofman writes, "Thanks to the concept, man arranges the whole universe into well-ordered categories without realizing that he is thus continuing the most archaic metaphorical activity."[17] The concept of, say, a leaf, when thought of nonmetaphorically, is misleading. Nietzsche writes:

> Every concept originates through our equating what is unequal. No leaf ever wholly equals another, and the concept "leaf" is formed through an arbitrary abstraction from these individual differences, through forgetting the distinction; and now it gives rise to the idea that in nature there might be something besides the leaves which would be "leaf"—some kind of original form after which all leaves have been woven, marked, copied, colored, curled, and painted, but by unskilled hands, so that no

copy turned out to be correct, reliable, and faithful image of the original form. (*TL*, 46)

The Socratic project of searching for stable and static knowledge succeeds only in reducing the strange and different "to the familiar" (*GS*, 355). "Look," Nietzsche writes, "isn't our need for knowledge precisely this need for the familiar, the will to uncover under everything strange, unusual, and questionable something that no longer disturbs us" (*GS*, 355)?

Improving by Dividing

In the remainder of this chapter, I discuss how, according to Nietzsche, Socrates' faith in reason implies and injects two nihilistic dualisms into the course of Western history. The first is a metaphysical dualism in which there emerges an apparent world, the world of Becoming, and a True world, the world of Being. In the Socratic worldview, this world of Becoming is thought to be devoid of significant meaning and value. The second dualism is anthropological. The human person is thought to be composed of a mind that reasons and a body that does not.

Nietzsche's critique of these dualisms points to one of our primary theses concerning his criticism of the Christian-moral interpretation—that it is connected to the attempt to sunder the interdependent and nonexclusive relationship between certain conceptual pairs of opposing qualities, labeled "positive" and "negative." Truth is opposed to appearance. Spirit or mind is opposed to corporeality. And only in a truth that is eternal, static, simple, and unhistorical is meaning present. The only access to this meaning is the disembodied, reasoning mind. As the body and the world are subject to change and decay, they are thought to be in error. These two dualisms pave the way for the apathy of the "last man."

The Tyranny of the True World and the Denigration of Appearance

Nietzsche's discussion of Socrates in *The Birth of Tragedy* centers on the role he and Euripides play in the transformation of an earlier culture built on a tragic and "pessimistic" but ultimately affirmative worldview to an "optimistic" but ultimately nihilistic one based on theoretical science. Central to this transformation is a shift in what is thought to constitute the sources of wisdom. Because Socrates saw ahistorical reason as the path to happiness, guaranteed only by stability, consistency, straightness, and Being, he implemented the process whereby the world of Becoming, with its Dionysian ambiguity and its composition of entities that "wander between the two poles of generation and decay," is ultimately rejected as a source of wisdom. This rejection amounts to the origination of an ontological distinction between the True world of Being and the Apparent world of Becoming.

With his "radical new admiration for knowledge" that is devoid of ambiguity, Socrates condemns the arts as containing only a mere instinct for, or simulation of, truth.

> "Only by instinct": with this phrase we touch upon the heart and core of the Socratic tendency. With it Socratism condemns existing art as well as existing ethics. Wherever Socratism turns its searching eyes it sees lack of insight and the power of illusion; and from this lack it infers the essential perversity and reprehensibility of what exists. (*BT*, 13)

Socrates and Euripides attempted to correct this situation, each with his respective medium. Illusory art is to be replaced by philosophical art or, better, by philosophy proper.

Euripides wrote tragedies on the basis of an "aesthetic Socratism," which has as its axiom the requirement that everything must be "intelligible" if it is to be considered "beautiful" (*BT*, 12). Beauty is, in this case, the simple and rational. It is Apollonian. Euripides followed Socrates' claim that ahistorical "reason was the true source of all enjoyment and creativity" (*BT*, 12). With this new principle, Euripides came to think that the tragic dramas of the preceding generation were nonrational and incommensurable in that they had "a certain deceptive precision and at the same time an enigmatic depth, an infinite background" (*BT*, 11). There was too much uncertainty and ambiguity in the early tragedies. Their "meaning" was anything but clear. Early tragedies were not simply tales about right and wrong. Good people often made out poorly, and evil often triumphed. This fact is what made them tragic. The early tragedies displayed individuals suffering from the tragic consequences of life in the world without necessarily resolving their problems. Nietzsche says that Euripides was troubled by this, thinking it to be a violation of what he assumed to be a moral universe.[18] "And how dubious the solution of

the ethical problems remained to him. . . . How irregular the distri-
bution of fortune and misfortune" (*BT,* 11)! "Even in the language of
the older tragedies," Nietzsche continues, Euripides "found much
that was repellent, or puzzling at the very least" (*BT,* 11). Euripides
claimed, in short, that Dionysianism, with its moral ambiguity,
should not be taken as the mark of ultimate reality. Euripides wanted
to correct and improve the art form. With his "aesthetic Socratism,"
"Euripides measured all the separate elements of the drama—language, characters, dramaturgic structure, and choric music—and corrected them according to this principle" (*BT,* 12).

To be sure, Euripides was not wrong in understanding the previous
generation of tragedies as amoral and "irrational." Where he faltered,
Nietzsche argues, is in his contention that ultimate reality is neither
amoral nor Dionysian. Hoping to straighten out the art form, Euripides
sought to eradicate the Dionysian elements, thus eliminating that which
made tragedy incommensurable with what he took to be reality.

> To separate this original and all-powerful Dionysian element from
> tragedy, and to reconstruct tragedy purely on the basis of an un-
> Dionysian art, morality, and world view—this is the tendency of Euripi-
> des as it now reveals itself to us in clear illumination. (*BT,* 12)

The chief laws of Socrates, which Euripides sought to implement
within his own form of tragedy, are that virtue is knowledge, that all
sins are the result of ignorance, and that the virtuous man is the happy
man (*BT,* 14). "In these three basic optimistic formulae," Nietzsche
writes, "lies the death of tragedy" (*BT,* 14).

In Nietzsche's estimation, the Euripidean tragedy became only a
teaching vehicle for a moral lesson. The Socratic-Euripidean worldview is one in which people ultimately get their just desserts. In the
early, pre-Euripidean tragedies, the audience was able to participate
in the drama and, through this participation, to be exposed to the
"eternal joy of becoming" (*TI,* "What I Owe to the Ancients," 5). The
Euripidean plays, in contrast, were viewed as vehicles for the moral
axioms thought to be necessary for overcoming ignorance. If art bestows any gifts in the Socratic world, it is only because it can be the
medium for delivering a moral message. It is not insignificant that
Socrates found Aesop's fables to be the only understandable form of
poetry. But now, with Euripides and his rational Socratic aesthetic, the
audience does not become immersed and involved in the world of

the work of art but is rather responsible for decoding the meaning of the drama, which is, at best, only symbolically meaningful. The meaning resides above, below, or behind the work of art. The aesthetic value of the play does not matter. The tragic drama itself is presumed to have no intrinsic meaning, being only a vehicle for a moral lesson. The message could just as easily be put and imparted in a number of different genres. Euripides is similar to one who looks at an abstract painting and complains that he cannot figure out what it signifies.

In the Socratic and Euripidean worldview, the physical world is construed along the same lines as the work of art. Like the tragic drama, the physical world does not have its own intrinsic value or meaning. As a mere realm of "particulars," the world merely hints and dimly points to the higher world of Forms. The world is an imperfect copy of the True world of Forms. The Particular, for Socrates, must not be mistaken for the Form.

When truth is defined ahistorically, the world of Becoming is seen as a place of mere appearance. As such, it is not the location or source of wisdom. For Socrates, the knowledge necessary for human existence is not in the world. Life in the world now becomes the project of hermeneutically decoding the Dionysian ambiguity and looking for its true meaning. Life, like the tragedy, is not to be participated in but coolly observed from the distance.

"Socrates," Nietzsche writes, "might be called the typical *non-mystic*, in whom, through a hypertrophy, the logical nature is developed as excessively as instinctive wisdom is in the mystic" (*BT*, 13). By attempting to remove the Dionysian elements of reality through ahistorical reason, Socrates removes our capacity for passion, awe, and the possibility for a creative and aesthetic existence. Life becomes a dull affair. This lack of awe can be seen in the fact that Socrates goes to his death with "complete clarity of mind and without any natural awe of death" (*BT*, 13). In the *Phaedo*, Socrates says "that those who really apply themselves in the right way to philosophy are directly and of their own accord preparing themselves for dying and death."[19] One is to be defensive and cautious while on this earth.

When "the *dying Socrates* becomes the new ideal for noble Greek youth" (*BT*, 13), life in the world becomes, in Nietzsche's eyes, only a sort of living death. When the dying Socrates, full of clarity and control, becomes the ideal for a culture, culture loses its health and natural creative power and humanity stands "stripped of myth, eternally starving" (*BT*, 23). Nietzsche imagines Socrates having only "one great Cyclops eye," which has been denied the pleasure of "gazing into the Dionysian abysses" (*BT*, 14). With only one eye, Nietzsche suggests, Socrates can no longer see with any depth and has no sense of the wonderful plasticity of reality.

For Nietzsche, as we will see in a later chapter, the ambiguous nature of the Dionysian reality, with its lack of static Truth, grants the person a life of play, childlikeness, and dance. Socrates required a certain defensive stance for life in the world. Only by saying No to appearance, the body, and Dionysus, thought Socrates, is one in a position to find Truth. All of this, Nietzsche argues, weakens and impoverishes the person. The aposematic stance of Socrates is unnecessary. Nietzsche wants to show that "having quills is a waste of time, even a double luxury, when one can choose not to have quills, but *open* hands" (*EH*, "Why I Am So Clever," 8). To have "open hands" is to take delight in affirming a world of appearances. Hayden White writes:

> Nietzsche's purpose as a philosopher was to transcend Irony by freeing consciousness from all Metonymical apprehensions of the world (which bred the doctrines of mechanical causality and a dehumanizing science) on the one hand and all Synecdochic sublimations of the world (which bred the doctrines of "higher" causes, gods spirits, and morality) on the other and to return consciousness to the enjoyment of its Metaphorical powers, its capacity to "frolic in images," to entertain the world as pure phenomena.[20]

The capacity to "frolic in images," with a certain childlikeness, is a fine description of what Nietzsche thought to be possible after the death of God.

Socrates and the Mind–Body Dualism

I now turn to the second dualism created by Socrates' faith in ahistorical reason as the key to improving the human situation. Because Socrates takes the acquisition of an ahistorical True knowledge to be the necessary and fundamental activity of "improving" the human condition, and because knowledge is True when and only if it is not limited by the boundaries of a particular, changing, historical body, Truth is not to be found in this world of appearance, bodies, and change. But Socrates is not, at least in his own eyes, a full-fledged epistemological nihilist, taking epistemological nihilism to mean, in Karen Carr's phrase, "the denial of the possibility of knowledge."[21] He does not maintain that we forever lack access to the ahistorical Truth. Here, though, epistemological nihilism is avoided only by putting forth a philosophical anthropology that recapitulates the metaphysical dualism of the True world of Being and the Apparent world of Becoming. The human person is thought to be composed of a soul and a body. The soul is immortal and "deathless," properly belonging to the True world of Being. The body, so fraught with change, is part of the world. Socrates avoids epistemological nihilism only by embracing two dualisms that are, in the end, imbued with the view that takes finite entities to be meaningless, to be without Truth.

For Socrates, one may tap into the fountain of Truth by pursuing philosophy with the soul (or mind). This entails turning away from a concern with things in the visible, physical world to the invisible world. It requires a turn inward.

> Don't you think [asks Socrates] that the person who is likely to succeed in this attempt most perfectly is the one who approaches each object, as far as possible, with the unaided intellect, without taking account of any sense of sight in his thinking, or dragging any other sense into his reckoning—the man who pursues the truth by applying his pure and unadulterated thought to the pure and unadulterated object, cutting himself off as much as possible from his eyes and ears and virtually all the rest of his body. . . . Is not this the person, Simmias, who will reach the goal of reality, if anybody can?[22]

For the soul to be successful, it must engage in a practice of asceticism that severs the influence the body has on the soul. The body is only a hindrance to the pursuit of Truth. Bodily desires and instincts must not influence the soul. The essence of the human person is the soul, and, by Socrates' understanding of the soul, this essence is unabashedly unworldly.

Because Socrates advocated the idea that we must have, in Nietzsche's words, "rationality at any price," reason is turned "into a tyrant" (*TI*, "The Problem of Socrates," 11). Reflecting on *The Birth of Tragedy* much later in *Ecce Homo*, Nietzsche states that one of the book's innovations was that it offered an understanding of "Socratism": "Socrates is recognized for the first time as an instrument of Greek disintegration, as a typical decadent. 'Rationality' *against* instinct. 'Rationality' at any price as a dangerous force that undermines

life" (*EH*, "The Birth of Tragedy," 1). Socrates supposes a hostility between the mind and the body. His faith in ahistorical reason pits the
soul against the other inspirations for action and sources of information about the world—namely, the body and the instincts. By privileging the mind over the body, he denigrates the meaning and significance of the body, with its instincts, passions, and senses.

Nietzsche suggests that the great appeal of Socrates in Greek culture was due to the fact that Greek society was suffering from an "anarchy of the instincts." "Everywhere one was within five paces of excess: *monstrum in animo* was the general danger" (*TI*, "The Problem
of Socrates," 9). To counter the threat of the instincts, Socrates advocated the use of reason as the cure, advancing the position that virtue
and happiness could not be found through the bodily instincts and
passions, but only through reason. Reason became a "counter-tyrant"
(*TI*, "The Problem of Socrates," 9).

> Reason-virtue-happiness, that means that one must imitate Socrates and
> counter the dark appetites with a permanent daylight—the daylight of
> reason. One must be clever, clear, bright at any price: any concession to
> the instincts, to the unconscious, leads *downward*. (*TI*, "The Problem of
> Socrates," 10)

It was Socrates' intention, therefore, to counter what he himself took
to be a form of decadence by negating the passions and instincts, in
short, the body, with the mind and its faculty of reason. But, Nietzsche
writes, Socrates was wrong to think this could bring about a solution
to the problems of Greek society.

> It is a self-deception on the part of the philosophers and moralists if
> they believe that they are extricating themselves from decadence when
> they merely wage war against it. Extrication lies beyond their strength:
> what they choose as a means, as salvation, is itself but another expres
> sion of decadence; they change its expression, but they do not get rid
> of decadence itself. (*TI*, "The Problem of Socrates," 11)

The attempt to wage war against what Socrates took to be a growing decadence amounts, in this case, to a war against the forces and
ways of the worldly. This war against the instincts takes part in the essential features of "improvement-morality." The attempt is made to
improve the human condition by removing something from the picture. In this case, the body and its instincts are to be denied. Nietzsche

does not disagree with Socrates' claim that the instincts of a human being need to be brought under some control. But if one attempts to remove or extirpate them, the problems are tremendous. This repudiation of the body and the instincts does a great deal, as we will see, for the "promotion" of the apathy of the last man. It is part of the process of the "taming" of and, what Nietzsche calls, the "un-selfing" of humanity. In sum, Socrates' distaste for the nature of this world prompted him to attempt to "improve" it. But Nietzsche thinks this "improvement" is accomplished only at the expense of turning away from the world. What we are left with is the view that no wisdom exists in the entities within the world of Becoming. Thus, accessing wisdom requires that we turn inward, away from the body and towards the soul. These biases are taken up by Christianity and, later, by Kantian philosophy, which I discuss in the next chapter.

NOTES

1. See Peter Berkowitz, *Nietzsche: The Ethics of an Immoralist* (Cambridge, Mass.: Harvard University Press, 1995), 69.

2. Walter Kaufmann argues that Nietzsche had a very favorable view of Socrates. See *Nietzsche: Philosopher, Psychologist, Antichrist*, 392–93. This view is, I think, mistaken. Before Nietzsche came to understand his thought as the contrast between Dionysus and the Crucified, he stated that Socrates was his antagonist. "This is the new opposition: the Dionysian and the Socratic" (*BT*, 12). In *Human, All Too Human*, Nietzsche does refer to Socrates positively, but in *The Twilight of Idols* he returns to his negative view.

3. In the *Phaedo* (in *The Collected Dialogues*, ed. Edith Hamilton and Huntington Cairns [Princeton, N.J.: Princeton University Press, 1961], section 66E), Plato has Socrates say, "It seems, to judge from the argument, that the wisdom which we desire and upon which we profess to have set our hearts will be attainable only when we are dead, and not in our lifetime."

4. Morgan, *What Nietzsche Means*, 212.

5. Plato, *The Republic*, in *The Collected Dialogues*, Book VII, section 515B.

6. Plato, *Republic*, Book VII, section 514A.

7. Plato, *Republic*, Book VI, section 485A; emphasis added.

8. Plato, *Republic*, Book VI, section 485C.

9. Plato, *Phaedo*, section 66D.

10. Plato, *Phaedo*, section 79D.

11. Manfred Riedel, "The 'Wondrous Double Nature' of Philosophy: Nietzsche's Determination of the Original Experience of Thinking among the

Greeks," *Graduate Faculty Philosophy Journal* (New School for Social Research) 15, no. 2 (1991): 50.

12. To be sure, Socrates is well aware of the interdependent relationship between certain opposing concepts. His argument for the immortality of the soul in the *Phaedo* begins with the idea that life and death give rise to one another.

> So we agree upon this too—that the living have come from the dead no less than the dead from the living. But I think we decided that if this was so, it was sufficient proof that the souls of the dead must exist in some place from which they are reborn. (*Phaedo*, section 72A)

But by the time Socrates is done proving the soul's immortality, the interdependence of opposing concepts is rejected for the view that the soul, because it is the principle of life, can never die. Here, Socrates relies on the view that life and death are related in such a way that pure life is directly opposed to death. "We maintain that the opposites themselves would absolutely refuse to tolerate coming into being from one another" (*Phaedo*, section 103C). For more on this see David Farrell Krell, *Infectious Nietzsche* (Bloomington: Indiana University Press, 1996), 94. Furthermore, even when Socrates entertains the idea that, for example, pain gives rise to pleasure, he still maintains that they are logically and ontologically different things, saying "they will never come to a man both at once" (*Phaedo*, section 60B). For Nietzsche, the relationship is such that it would be possible to experience both sensations at the same time. In fact, such an experience is what creates the possibility of tragic art. In *The Will to Power*, Nietzsche writes that the "highest and most illustrious human joys" come when "an overflowing wealth of the most multifarious forces and the most dextrous power of 'free willing' and lordly command dwell amicably together in one man" (*WP*, 1051; 1885).

13. Plato, *Phaedo*, section 83B.

14. Plato, *Phaedo*, section 117E.

15. This interpretation of Nietzsche's famous hypothesis concerning the femininity of truth is in tension with other, perhaps misogynistic, statements made by him concerning women. In this work, I do not want either to confirm or discount what may in fact be a misogynistic strain in Nietzsche's work. For more on Nietzsche's view of women, see the essays in *Nietzsche and the Feminine*, ed. Peter Burgard (Charlottesville: University of Virginia Press, 1994).

16. Richard Schacht, *Making Sense of Nietzsche: Reflections Timely and Untimely* (Urbana: University of Illinois Press, 1995), 47.

17. Sarah Kofman, *Nietzsche and Metaphor*, trans. Duncan Large (Stanford, Calif.: Stanford University Press, 1993), 35.

18. The illogical nature of Aeschylus's plays, as Martha Nussbaum reports, still troubles some contemporary critics. See *The Fragility of Goodness: Luck*

and Ethics in Greek Tragedy and Philosophy (Cambridge: Cambridge University Press, 1986), 26.

19. Plato, *Phaedo,* section 64A.

20. Hayden White, *Metahistory: The Historical Imagination in Nineteenth Century Europe* (Baltimore: Johns Hopkins University Press, 1973), 334.

21. Karen L. Carr, *The Banalization of Nihilism: Twentieth-Century Responses to Meaninglessness* (Albany: State University of New York Press, 1992), 17.

22. Plato, *Phaedo*, sections 65E–66A.

4

The Rise and Development
of the Christian-Moral
Interpretation, Part 2

Christianity and Kantian Philosophy

According to Nietzsche, the Socratic conception of ahistorical reason, the distaste for things Dionysian, the denigration of the Body, and, most notably, the belief in a "True World of Being" become the foundation of Western intellectual history. In this chapter, my concern is to show how the devaluation of the meaning and value of human life in the world is continued and refined by Christianity and Kantian philosophy.

CHRISTIANITY

Christianity has cheated us out of the harvest of ancient culture.

—*Nietzsche*, The Antichrist

Nihilism and Christianism: that rhymes, that does not only rhyme.[1]

—*Nietzsche*, The Antichrist

Christianity and Socratic-Platonism are, for Nietzsche, two kindred movements, one emerging out of the other. Plato is "pre-existently Christian" (*TI*, "What I Owe to the Ancients," 2). In fact, Christianity, for Nietzsche, "is Platonism for 'the people'" (*BGE*, preface).[2]

Although aspects of Nietzsche's criticism of Christianity revolve around the stance that many of its claims are philosophically untenable,[3] he is much more concerned with the ethical ramifications of

Christianity, meaning that he is concerned with the sort of practices engendered by the Christian worldview and values. Because Christianity is so thoroughly concerned with elaborating the way in which human life is ultimately meaningful, Nietzsche knows he would be hard-pressed to indict Christianity with the sort of nihilism that purports human life to be absolutely meaningless. His criticism of Christianity flows from a simple formula:

> What is good? Everything that heightens the feeling of power in man, the will to power, power itself.
>
> What is bad? Everything that is born of weakness.
>
> What is happiness? The feeling that power is *growing*, that resistance is overcome.
>
> Not contentedness but more power; not peace but war. (*A*, 2)

As Nietzsche understands it, Christianity is bad in the sense that it does not heighten the feeling of power; it does not increase one's desire to affirm worldly life. Rather, as Nietzsche states, Christianity displays an "active pity for all the failures and all the weak" (*A*, 2). It is hostile to life. Describing this sentiment towards the Christian concept of God, Nietzsche writes:

> That we find no God—either in history or in nature or behind nature— is not what differentiates *us*, but that we experience what has been revered as God, not as "godlike" but as miserable, as absurd, as harmful, not merely as an error but as a *crime against life*. We deny God as God. (*A*, 47)

Christianity preaches, Nietzsche thinks, the necessity of withdrawing from life in the world.

> Formerly, the proof of man's higher origin, of his divinity, was found in his consciousness, in his "spirit." To become *perfect*, he was advised to draw in his senses, turtle fashion, to cease all intercourse with earthly things, to shed his mortal shroud: then his essence would remain, the "pure spirit." (*A*, 14)

To become authentic, one must rid oneself of his or her earthly nature. It is not, in the end, worldly and bodily life that is affirmed by Christianity.

Nietzsche indicts the meaning attributed to human life by Christianity as nihilistic because that meaning comes only in the form of a *promise* to be fulfilled in another world. For the Christian, life in the world is justified as only a path to a greater reality (*WP*, 1052; 1888). In this way, meaning is deferred to a future moment after and beyond earthly existence. The second stage in Nietzsche's "history of an error," the history and development of the notion of a "True World," refers to Christianity.

> The true world—unattainable for now, but promised for the sage, the pious, the virtuous man ("for the sinner who repents").
>
> (Progress of the idea: it becomes more subtle, insidious, incomprehensible—*it becomes female*, it becomes Christian). (*TI*, "How the 'True World' Finally Became a Fable")

For Nietzsche, the virtuous and pious Christian is one who forsakes a sense of strength and active life in this world on the promise of some future tomorrow in a world beyond this one. For Nietzsche, because there is no "beyond," this is an empty promise. "When one places life's center of gravity not in life but in the 'beyond'—*in nothingness*—one deprives life of its center of gravity altogether" (*A*, 43).

The Rewriting of History and the
Deferral and Displacement of Meaning

In the previous chapter, we saw that the worldview advocated and advanced by Socratic-Platonism was one that privileged the categories of Being over those of Becoming. In the case of Socrates, this preference—which attempted to privilege Apollo over Dionysus—allowed him to make a case for the ahistorical rationality of ultimate reality. The consequence of this interpretation is that the world becomes a mere signpost for the world of Forms. For Socrates, the changing and chaotic world of Becoming is, in itself, of no value because it lacks stability and cannot, therefore, be a source of Truth. It must be hermeneutically decoded.

The devaluing of the world of Becoming by means of this sort of interpretation continues in Christianity. In Christianity, it occurs by means of something Nietzsche calls the "moral world order."

> What does "moral world order" mean? That there is a will of God, once and for all, as to what man is to do and what he is not to do; that the value of a people, of an individual, is to be measured according to how much or how little the will of God is obeyed. (*A*, 26)

Measuring the meaning and value of entities and actions by the standard of the "will of God" removes, or at least weakens, any possible
intrinsic value an act or entity might contain. "In short, everything that
contains its value *in itself* is made altogether valueless. . . . [N]ow it requires a sanction after the event" (*A*, 26). In an aphorism written at
least seven years before *The Antichrist*, Nietzsche describes how for
Pascal everything that happened to his body—"the beating of the
heart, the nerves, the bile, the semen"—"had to be seen . . . as a moral
and religious phenomenon, and he had to ask whether God or Devil
. . . was to be discovered in them" (*D*, 86)!

The way in which Christianity accomplishes the translation of the
intrinsic meaning of worldly entities and events into the moral world
order is by means of a particular interpretation of the life and death of
Jesus Christ. In a manner that might strike some as surprising, Nietzsche, at least in *The Antichrist*, exhibits a tender respect toward Jesus himself:

> He never had any reason to negate "the world"; the ecclesiastical con-
> cept of "world" never occurred to him. To negate is the very thing that
> is impossible for him. Dialectic is equally lacking; the very idea is lack-
> ing that a faith, a "truth," might be proved by reasons. (*A*, 32)

As in the case of Nietzsche's noble individuals, Jesus' "proofs are inner 'lights,' inner feelings of pleasure and self-affirmations, all of them
'proofs of strength'" (*A*, 32). Jesus needed no external verification or
proof on which to base his actions. They were derived from an inner
conviction. Although Jesus is a decadent in Nietzsche's eyes, his actions are not fueled by a spirit of *ressentiment*. Jesus achieves a sort
of happiness within reality. In Peter Berkowitz's words: "Rather than
teach a faith, Jesus showed how to experience eternity within the
confines of finite human life."[4]

In Christian theology, the life and death of Jesus Christ came to be
used as a *proof*, a hermeneutical key to the new "meaning" of the
world. The translation of the meaning of the world into the "moral
world order" is accomplished, for the most part, by Paul and the first
disciples. They interpreted the life and death of Jesus as "proof" for
the authority of the "moral world order." Nietzsche argues that Paul
rewrites the history of Jesus' life and death so that it becomes the story
of a promise and hope for a better life in the beyond. "The life, the example, the doctrine, the death, the meaning and the right of the en-

tire evangel—nothing remained once this hate-inspired counterfeiter realized what alone he could use. *Not* the reality, *not* the historical truth" (*A*, 42).

This rewriting of history, Nietzsche claims, is a continuation of the same crime against history committed by the Jewish priests who rewrote and falsified the history of Israel as an attempt at securing their own power within the community. The result of this reinterpretation is that the source of value and meaning in Jewish life—namely God, is *denatured*. Originally, Nietzsche asserts, Israel had conceived a picture of Yahweh that was "the expression of a consciousness of power, of joy in oneself, of hope for oneself" (*A*, 25).[5] God is natural insofar as God is a sign of strength. This early phase of Israel's history, Nietzsche argues, is the expression of a culture that knew itself to be powerful and noble and had, therefore, a natural and healthy relationship to the divine.

This natural and life-affirming relationship to God was destroyed as Israel began to experience internal and external strife. Even after Israel's situation in the world changed, the people still retained their notion of God. But because the community was no longer as strong as it had been in the past, God became more of an ideal than a live, strong, and life-affirming concept. "The people, however, clung to the vision, as the highest desirability" (*A*, 25).

Israel's situation worsens, Nietzsche continues, and this conception of God begins to fail as the hopes of Israel go unfulfilled. "The old god was no longer able to do what he once could do" (*A*, 25). At this point, for Nietzsche, the ideal or concept of God should have been abandoned. Instead of being abandoned altogether, however, the concept is merely revised. But this time it is at the expense of "denaturing" it. God is no longer conceived as one with Israel but is given a position transcendent to the world. All happiness experienced in the community of Israel is no longer seen to be the result of its power but is now thought to be only a reward for obedience. Unhappiness is interpreted as punishment for disobedience. Here enters, for Nietzsche, a crucial concept in the history of Judaism and the Western world: sin. Nietzsche writes that sin is "that most mendacious device of interpretation, the alleged 'moral world order'" (*A*, 25). God is no longer a God who helps and inspires but a God who demands obedience.

This marks the transition from an idea of God that would enhance reverence for life in the world to a God who can promote only weakness and hatred of reality. The notion of sin and the act of denaturalizing God allows the priest to procure power within the community. The concept of sin requires a concept of forgiveness, which in turn requires the concept of a priest. "Supreme principle: 'God forgives those who repent'— in plain language: those who submit to the priest" (*A*, 26). If the concepts of sin and guilt can be accepted by the community, the priest then becomes the instrument by which this forgiveness can be implemented.

For the community to accept the idea of sin and guilt, the priests must rewrite the history of Israel. They must create a picture of the past that shows it to be a history of Israel's obedient and disobedient relations to God. The actual history of Israel could not be used. It had to be falsified.

> With matchless scorn for every tradition, for every historical reality, they translated the past of their own people into religious terms, that is, they turned it into a stupid salvation mechanism of guilt before Yahweh, and punishment; of piety before Yahweh, and reward. (*A*, 26)

The once great and powerful Israel of the past is rewritten so that it resembles an "age of decay" and "long misfortune" (*A*, 26). Events that might have served in a "monumental history" are rewritten to be a history of weakness.

The priest secures power by rewriting the history of Israel so that it becomes a story of rewards and punishments for, respectively, adhering to the will of God and going against it. This rewritten history then gets touted as "holy scripture." For Nietzsche, it amounts to a piece of propaganda that hopes to convince the community that what it says about God represents the way Israel has always understood God. "The 'will of God' had long been fixed; all misfortune rests on one's having become estranged from the 'holy scripture'" (*A*, 26). As "holy scripture," it fixes the perspective of the past so that no other perspective can be entertained.

Nietzsche's purpose in laying out the process by which the Old Testament was produced is twofold. First, he wants to show that Christianity is a continuation of the Jewish act of denaturalizing the sources of meaning and value by relegating them to a transcendent realm. Christianity re-presents and reenacts priestly interests. Nietzsche sees Paul and the other first Christians as merely carrying on this process of securing power and devaluating of nature. The other reason is that an understanding of Christianity, for Nietzsche, can only be achieved by understanding the culture out of which it grew. The following captures both of Nietzsche's concerns: "Christianity can be understood only in terms of the soil out of which it grew—it is *not* a counter-movement to the Jewish instinct, it is its very consequence, one inference more in its awe-inspiring logic" (*A*, 24). Paul's explanation of the meaning of Jesus' life and death is identical to the priestly rewriting of history: "And once more the priestly instinct of the Jew committed the same great crime against history—he simply crossed out the yesterday of Christianity and its day before yesterday; he *invented his own history of earliest Christianity*" (*A*, 42). The purpose of this falsification is again the acquisition of power, which Paul attempts by the same means as the priests: by devaluing what for Nietzsche is the natural world.

The Christian devaluation of nature is accomplished by re-presenting Jesus' life and death as a rebellion against the existing ruling order. According to Nietzsche, the followers of Jesus were themselves involved in a revolt against the ruling Jewish order, and with the death of Christ, they were faced with questions pertaining to the identity and nature of Christ. To cope with these questions and also to avoid the possibility that the execution of Christ entailed the refutation of their own cause, the disciples found it necessary to ascribe a reason and meaning to the crucifixion. From here, Nietzsche says, came the question "who killed him?" To this they answered: the ruling Jewry. Reminiscent of Euripides' intolerance for tragedies that do not end with a rational and moral resolution, the first disciples could not accept Jesus' death without a "reason." "Here everything *had* to be necessary, had to have meaning, reason, the highest reason; a disciple's love knows no accident" (*A*, 40). Unable to forgive the death, feelings of *ressentiment* in the disciples gave rise to the concepts "retribution," "judgment," and "kingdom of God." The idea of a kingdom of God, therefore, turns the meaning of Jesus' life and death into a promise for the future. Here, for Nietzsche, is Christianity's prime means of devaluing nature and denaturing value. "But in this way everything is misunderstood: the 'kingdom of God' as the last act, as a promise! After all, the evangel had been precisely the presence, the fulfillment, the *reality* of this 'kingdom'" (*A*, 40). The invocation of the concept of "promise" has the effect of severing what Nietzsche takes to be Jesus' real message of the very presence of the kingdom of God, and putting in its place the idea of promise and hope for a future kingdom of God in an existence beyond the present one. The present life is thereby devalued.

The overall result of this is that in Christian practice, in the life of faith, one must always keep one's eyes on the future. In "the case of the ascetic life, life counts as a bridge to that other mode of existence. The ascetic treats life as a wrong road on which one must finally walk back to the point where it begins, or as a mistake that is put right by deeds" (*GM*, III:11). One is not to live in the present because it is presumed that the meaning of life is to come after life. "To live so, that there is no longer any sense in living, that now become the 'sense' of life" (*A*, 43). The value and meaning of the world is now to be determined by the standard of the "moral world order." Entities and actions are adjudicated on the basis of their adherence to God's will. Not only does the notion of the "moral world order" take away the possibility that life in the world is intrinsically meaningful, but, because God is transcendent, the value of the world is measured by an unworldly and unnatural standard.

The Denigration of the Natural,
the Practice of Pity, and the Desire for Comfort

> Then, during the moral epoch of mankind, one sacrificed to one's god one's own strongest instincts, one's "nature": *this* festive joy lights up the cruel eyes of the ascetic, the "anti-natural" enthusiast.
>
> —*Nietzsche,* Beyond Good and Evil

By placing the center and meaning of existence in the "beyond," in God, Christianity requires, as Nietzsche sees it, a turn away from this world and what is natural to it. Christianity places the essence of the human being in a soul or spirit that is thought to be "pure." Purity refers to that which does not traffic with the soil and the earth, that which is bodiless and thus, without instincts, desires, and self-interests. In Christian practice, the "body is despised" (*A*, 21).

> Wherever the teaching of *pure spirituality* has ruled, it has destroyed nervous energy with its excesses: it has taught deprecation, neglect, or tormenting of the body and men to torment and deprecate themselves on account of the drives which fill them. (*D*, 39)

Nietzsche offers a psychological explanation for the Christian distaste for the body and the natural. "It was the sick and decaying who despised body and earth and invented the heavenly realm and the redemptive drops of blood" (*Z*, I:3). In other words, the teachers of "pure spirituality" were, like Socrates, decadent.

In the previous chapter, I showed how Socrates begins the campaign for an anthropology that viewed the material body as unessential and accidental. This anthropology gained credibility by means of the belief in a dualistic cosmology that described the realm of ultimate reality as one that has only the qualities of Being and none of the qualities of Becoming. Christianity participates in this campaign, though with a slightly different focus. In Christianity, the idea of "pure spirit" is propagated through what Nietzsche calls the "slave revolt" in morality. This revolt is largely an attempt at overturning a morality that is rooted in the body, the instincts, a sense of strength, and a natural feeling of well-being, which Nietzsche calls "master," "noble," "aristocratic," and "knightly" morality. The deepest quality of these nobles is self-reverence and a feeling of superiority.[6] In master morality, the selflessness of pure spirituality is entirely absent.

> Noble and courageous human beings . . . are furthest removed from that morality which finds the distinction of morality precisely in pity, or in acting for others, or in *desinteressement*; faith in oneself, pride in oneself, a fundamental hostility and irony against "selflessness" belong just as definitely to noble morality as does a slight disdain and caution regarding compassionate feelings and a "warm heart." (*BGE*, 260)

In contrast, the slavish type, who does not have a natural sense of strength and well-being, suffers in a world ruled by master morality. They lack all of the qualities that are revered as good. To make a life for themselves, they attempt to put in place a system of morality that does not find goodness in the qualities of the masters. The ascetic ideal (which is the ideal of the slavish type) "springs from the protective instinct of a degenerating instinct" (*GM*, III:13). The slavish type attempts to pronounce egoism, selfishness, and the other traits of masterly morality as *evil*. In turn, slave morality advocates selflessness, gentleness, and pity.

> Those qualities are brought out and flooded with light which serves to ease existence for those who suffer: here pity, the complaisant and obliging hand, the warm heart, patience, industry, humility, and friendliness are honored—for here these are the most useful qualities and almost the only means for enduring the pressure of existence. (*BGE*, 260)

The intention of this system of morality is to make existence gentler, kinder, and tamer. It is an effort to improve it for those who suffer from it and cannot live in it as it is. By advocating benevolence and pity, it seeks to reduce struggle and tension. It wants to make courage and strength qualities that are not only unnecessary for the good life but actually antitheses to it. The way in which it accomplishes this is by constructing the master as an enemy. This enemy allows the slavish type to project his or her dissatisfactions onto something outside of the self. This other, the enemy, is deemed "evil." "'The enemy' as the man of *ressentiment* conceives him—and here precisely is his deed, his creation: he has conceived 'the evil enemy,' '*the Evil One*'" (*GM*, I:10). By labeling them as evil, they are making the claim that the qualities exemplified by the masters are in opposition to what is True and Good in an absolute sense.

Evil qualities are those that are claimed to have no proper place within ultimate reality. In turn, it is assumed that ultimate reality is constituted only by the "good" qualities. This scheme goes against Nietzsche's claim that opposing concepts are interrelated; good can exist only in relation to its opposite. In contrast to the slavish scheme of *good and evil* is the masterly scheme of *good and bad*. The master certainly experiences certain events and entities with disfavor. But the master's reaction to these things is clearly different from the slave's reaction to evil. The master interprets these things as "bad," not "evil." When faced with the "bad," the master is not governed by the feeling of *ressentiment*. This is possible because the strong masterly type is not "reactive," meaning that the master does not draw his or her sense of self from something that exists outside the self.

> The "well-born" *felt* themselves to be the "happy"; they did not have to establish their happiness artificially by examining their enemies, or to persuade themselves, *deceive* themselves, that they were happy (as all men of *ressentiment* are in the habit of doing). (*GM*, I:10)

The master is capable of forgetting and shrugging off unpleasant experiences. "To be incapable of taking one's enemies, one's accidents, even one's misdeeds seriously for very long—that is the sign of strong, full natures" (*GM*, I:10). In short, the differences between the scheme of *good and evil* and *good and bad* reside in the conceived relationship between conceptual pairs. In the scheme of *good and evil*, it is thought that the Good is capable of existing in its own right, standing alone. The "evil" has no existence in "authentic" and eminent reality.

The results of these efforts to achieve a life of the "good" alone are disastrous, bringing about, says Nietzsche, nothing less than nihilism. A political order designed to reduce the amount of struggle between its constituents by making all people equal—here, Nietzsche is thinking of democracy and communism—"would be a principle *hostile to life*, an agent of the dissolution and destruction of man, an attempt to assassinate the future of man, a sign of weariness, a secret path to nothingness" (*GM*, II:11). It can produce only "tame" human beings who are mediocre and insipid. The tame human being is the one who attempts to remove all those qualities that seem distasteful or harmful. But these qualities can only be removed at great expense; they can be removed only by removing oneself from worldly life. The slavish individual, the Christian, can survive and implement this morality only by propagating a lie—"not *wanting* to see at any price how reality is constituted fundamentally" (*EH*, "Why I Am a Destiny," 4). Reality, for Nietzsche, is wrought with tension, struggle, suffering, cruelty, and aggression. It is amoral. Christian morality considers these aspects "as an objection, [things] that must be abolished" (*EH*, "Why I Am a Destiny," 4).

One of the ways in which Christianity attempts to abolish these aspects is through the practice of pity. Through pity we feel sorry for one who is in distress. But in this stance we are, Nietzsche thinks, practicing nihilism (*A*, 7). "Pity," he writes, "stands opposed to the tonic emotions which heighten our vitality: it has a depressing effect" (*A*, 7). Essentially, the pitying person tries to remove those qualities of a human life that "seduce" and invite one to have a life of creative and life-affirming willing. To pity others, to work for the removal of their suffering, is based on a lack of understanding of "the whole economy of the soul and the balance effected by 'distress.'" They "wish to *help*," Nietzsche continues,

> and have no thought of the personal necessity of distress, and although terrors, deprivations, impoverishments, midnights, adventures, risks, and blunders are as necessary for me and for you as are their opposites. It never occurs to them that, to put it mystically, the path to one's heaven always leads through the voluptuousness of one's own hell. (*GS*, 338)

"The terrible aspects of reality," he says, "are to an incalculable degree more necessary than that petty happiness which people call 'goodness'" (*EH*, "Why I Am a Destiny," 4).

As a religion of pity, Christianity is a "religion of comfortableness" (*GS*, 338) and in search of "improvement." Comfort can be achieved only at the expense of vital life. Christianity and democracy are, Nietzsche states, attempts at unbending the bow, by which he means they are attempts at reducing the tension necessary for shooting towards "the most distant goals" (*BGE*, preface). Pity is the seduction to nothingness (*GM*, preface, 5). In the next chapter, I will have more to say about the necessity of avoiding "comfort."

In sum, Christianity, for Nietzsche, amounts to a fight against the healthy and strong. It "has sided with all that is weak and base, with all failures; it has made an ideal of whatever *contradicts* the instinct of the strong life to preserve itself" (*A*, 5). It is an attempt to "un-self" the individual, teaching, he writes,

> man to despise the very first instincts of life; that one mendaciously invented a "soul," a "spirit" to ruin the body; that one taught men to experience the presupposition of life, sexuality, as something unclean; that one looks for the evil principle in what is most profoundly necessary for growth, in *severe* self-love (this very word constitutes slander); that, conversely, one regards the typical signs of decline and contradiction of the instincts, the "selfless," the loss of a center of gravity, "depersonalization" and "neighbor love" . . . as the *higher* value. (*EH*, "Why I Am a Destiny," 7)

KANTIAN PHILOSOPHY AND
THE UNSELFING OF HUMANITY

As I stated in the beginning of this chapter, Nietzsche argues that Christianity locates the essence of the human being in the "pure spirit." This "pure spirit" is thought to be unrelated to the body. Nietzsche often writes of Kant in the context of the dangers of the pure spirit or subject. Kant's philosophy, Nietzsche thinks, strengthened the spirit of disinterest and "objectivity" that began with Socrates' turn away from the body. Actions or values that were tinged with self-interest or subjectivity were thought to be lacking in moral caliber and less than truthful. Nietzsche sounds a warning against this view. "In the end we also have to learn caution against our gratitude and put a halt to the exaggerated manner in which the 'unselfing' and depersonalization of the spirit is being celebrated nowadays" (*BGE*, 207).

With this point in mind, Nietzsche takes Kant's categorical imperative as the "very recipe for decadence, even for idiocy" (*A*, 11). The ideas of a good-in-itself and universal (noncontextual) notions of virtue and duty are "chimeras and expressions of decline, of the final exhaustion of life" (*A*, 11). They make duty impersonal. Nietzsche does not dismiss notions of duty and virtue but only suggests that they must be personal discoveries. Regarding Kant, he says:

> Yet this nihilist with his Christian dogmatic entrails considered pleasure an *objection*. What could destroy us more quickly than working, thinking, and feeling without any inner necessity, without any deeply personal choice, without pleasure—as an automaton of "duty?" (*A*, 11)

For Nietzsche, the result of this is a general weakening of the human personality.[7]

Along similar lines, Nietzsche takes Kant's aesthetics to lead to the same sort of weakening of human personality. For Kant, Nietzsche quotes, the beautiful is that "which gives us pleasure *without interest*" (*GM*, III:6). Nietzsche is amused by this, writing, "If . . . one can *even* view undraped female statues 'without interest,' one may laugh a little at their expense" (*GM*, III:6). Contemplation without interest is a "nonsensical absurdity" (*GM*, III:12). Nietzsche offers Stendhal's idea of beauty as a contrast to Kant's disinterested aesthetic. Stendhal "calls the beautiful *une promesse de bonheur*," which ought to "arouse the will" (*GM*, III:6).

In Schopenhauer, Nietzsche finds a manifestation of the Kantian aesthetic that brings its nihilism into clear light. Making use of the Kantian notion of disinterested beauty, Schopenhauer finds aesthetic contemplation to be "lupulin and camphor," a sort of anesthesia for the will. Asking us to listen to its tone and sentiment, Nietzsche quotes Schopenhauer:

> This is the painless condition that Epicurus praised as the highest good and the condition of the gods; for a moment we are delivered from the vile urgency of the will; we celebrate the Sabbath of the penal servitude of volition; the wheel of Ixion stands still! (*GM*, III:6)

Schopenhauer thought that the beautiful should calm the will, and, by calming it, the human being can find a degree of relief.

Not far down the road from this point in intellectual history is Nietzsche's "last man," who no longer desires anything. To be sure, there is a difference between the last man and the human being Kant envisioned as governed by the categorical imperative. But insofar as Kant relegated the sphere of meaningfulness to the sphere of the noumena, he made such a realm ultimately unavailable. If such a person were to live according to the Kantian worldview, with a high degree of honesty, he or she would resemble, as Nietzsche writes, the German writer Heinrich von Kleist. In 1811, Kleist committed suicide. His desire to live was diminished earlier when his conviction that the world was meaningful, purposeful, and knowable was shattered by Kant's epistemology. Nietzsche writes in *Schopenhauer as Educator* that Kleist suffered from a "despair of truth" (*SE*, 3). This danger, he continues, "accompanies every thinker whose starting point is Kantian philosophy" (*SE*, 3). Nietzsche then goes on to quote a letter from Kleist:

> A short while ago . . . I became acquainted with Kant's philosophy—and I must now share with you one of his ideas, whereby I dare not fear that it will shatter you as deeply and painfully as it did me. We cannot decide whether what we call truth is really truth, or whether it only appears to us to be such. If the latter is the case, then the truth we collect here is nothing upon our death, and all our efforts to procure a possession that will follow us to the grave are in vain. . . . My sole, my supreme aim has disappeared, and I have no other. (*SE*, 3)

In the case of Kleist, epistemological nihilism gives way to the full-fledged despair of existential nihilism.

But, for those who are not as intellectually honest as Kleist, the life of the last man is a tempting alternative. The last man lives in a Kantian universe, but with some exceptions. Like Kant, he is no longer interested in any self-centered accomplishments, for he knows the realm of phenomena has little to offer. But unlike Kant, the last man no longer has the faith that if we wait this life out, there will be rewards in a later life. No longer capable of believing in God, the *noumena*, or the True World of Being, but still operating on the value system of the Christian-moral interpretation, the last man seeks merely to avoid as much pain, discomfort, and conflict as possible.

NOTES

1. In English the rhyme is a bit awkward. The German reads, "Nihilist und Christ: das reimt sich, das reimt sich nicht bloß."

2. Nietzsche, of course, is neither ignorant of nor silent about Christianity's Hebraic roots. In *The Antichrist* the genetic connection between Judaism and Christianity gives Nietzsche much food for thought.

3. Richard Schacht discusses some of these aspects in *Nietzsche* (Routledge: New York, 1983), 119–30.

4. Peter Berkowitz, *Nietzsche: The Ethics of an Immoralist* (Cambridge, Mass.: Harvard University Press, 1995), 113.

5. Nietzsche's own history of Israel, which spans sections 25 and 26 of *The Antichrist*, is brief, quick paced, and undocumented. It is important and interesting to note that it bears many similarities to Jules Wellhausen's *Prolegomena to the History of Ancient Israel*, which was published ten years before Nietzsche's *Antichrist*. Wellhausen argues that the Law must have been composed at a later date and that it was only during the exile that Judaism became a religion of law and ritual. For more on the connection between Nietzsche and Wellhausen, see Gary Shapiro, *Nietzschean Narratives* (Bloomington: Indiana University Press, 1989), 128–29.

6. See George Allan Morgan, *What Nietzsche Means* (Cambridge, Mass.: Harvard University Press, 1941; New York: Harper Torchbooks, 1965), 156.

7. See Gregory Bruce Smith, *Nietzsche, Heidegger, and the Transition to Postmodernity* (Chicago: University of Chicago Press, 1996), 88.

5

Nietzsche and the Life of Affirmation

> Did not the world become perfect just now? Round and Ripe?
>
> —*Nietzsche*, Thus Spoke Zarathustra

> But we have no wish whatever to enter into the kingdom of heaven: we have become men—*so we want the earth*.
>
> —*Nietzsche,* Thus Spoke Zarathustra

Up to this point, I have been discussing Nietzsche's understanding of the death of God and his criticism of Christianity. Although Nietzsche has received a good deal of attention as a critic of Western intellectual history, these efforts cannot be completely comprehended unless one understands that accompanying these efforts is a positive vision of the sort of possibilities for human life that are now available in the world. Or, as Nietzsche might put it, his task as a philosopher is comprised of both a "No-saying" and a "Yes-saying" (see *EH*, "Beyond Good and Evil," 1). Exclusive attention on Nietzsche's "No-saying" has led many critics to see Nietzsche as an "existential nihilist." But this is not an accurate statement because for Nietzsche, the death of God does not bring about a situation that necessarily leads to despair or apathy. In fact, Nietzsche often thought of his purpose as a philosopher to teach the possibilities of affirming worldly life. Our inability to affirm worldly life is due, Nietzsche thinks, to the Christian-moral interpretation, which leaves no room for a positive affirmation of the world of Becoming. The purpose of this chapter is to discuss how Nietzsche thinks it is possible for a human being to make life meaningful in a godless world.

Nietzsche called his philosophy "tragic wisdom"; it is tragic in the sense that it recognizes the fact that we live in a godless world, where suffering is ubiquitous, all that is created is destroyed, and there is no extraworldly redemption from this life. It is also wisdom in that the awareness of these facts is not simply something we "know" and must endure. Rather, Nietzsche's philosophy teaches that there are real possibilities for affirming life in the world. Tragic wisdom is a philosophy that recognizes the tragedy of life, while also showing a way of affirming this life within its tragedy. Nietzsche's philosophy is, as David Krell writes, "the affirmation of tragedy and the tragedy of affirmation."[1] We must be able to say Yes in such a way that "nothing in existence [is] subtracted" (*EH*, "The Birth of Tragedy," 2). In short, Nietzsche's proposal is to have us learn to live without God, which means learning to live in a world devoid of the values it was previously thought to have. Human beings are not created by God, the course of history is not divinely driven, sin is not the cause of suffering, and all Becoming is not kept in check by an ontologically superior realm of Being. But in the midst of this seemingly pessimistic picture, Nietzsche has ideas about a life that is more than mere acceptance. The one who overcomes nihilism, he thinks, can do more with existence than courageously accept and endure a life that seems to be at such odds with his or her needs. The life of the "last man" is not the only option. Rather, he wants to show that the death of God provides opportunities for human beings to realize their true potential as artists or value creators. For Nietzsche, the death of God is good news. There are, he thinks, real opportunities for *affirming* our existence.

For Nietzsche, the figure of Dionysus best embodies the sort of worldly affirmations he most admired. Dionysus represents "the tremendous, unbounded saying Yes and Amen" and carries this Yes-saying "into all abysses" (*EH*, "Thus Spoke Zarathustra," 6). In the remainder of this chapter, I would like to fill out these comments on Dionysus with some of Nietzsche's other discussions about what this affirmation entails and how it is possible.

THE EARLY GREEKS

Given Nietzsche's criticism of Christianity as an "improvement moral-ity," it should be no surprise that the first step in affirming worldly life is a new interpretation of the status of suffering, distress, and what have been called the "negative" qualities. If happiness, beauty, and the like, are not separable from their opposites, then affirming life in the world as meaningful involves a sort of "pessimism" con-cerning the hope of eradicating those things that cause distress. For Nietzsche, a courageous honesty concerning this "pessimistic" view is one of the crucial components to a nonnihilistic, affirmative world-view. Nietzsche suggests, in a series of rhetorical questions, that this sort of "pessimism" is actually a sign of strength, health, abundance, and affirmation. "Is there a pessimism of *strength?* An intellectual predilection for what is hard, terrible, evil, problematic in existence, arising from well-being, overflowing health, the abundance of exis-tence?" (*BT,* "Attempt at a Self-Criticism," 1). The problem with Chris-tianity is that it takes the existence of suffering to be a problem that needs to be overcome. Christianity offers a solution to suffering.[2] In Nietzsche's affirmative philosophy, suffering and the other negative qualities are not construed as things that are need of some solution. "To consider distress of all kinds as an objection, as something that must be abolished, is the *niaiserie par excellence* and, on a large scale, a veritable disaster in its consequences" (*EH,* "Why I Am a Des-tiny," 4). Such a stance requires, as we have said, a justification of the world in which we live.

Nietzsche was drawn to, and inspired by, ancient pre-Socratic Greek culture, from which he discerned an alternative way and view of life to the one he was offered in nineteenth-century European culture. In the Greek culture between Homer and Socrates—in "those centuries when the Greek body flourished and the Greek soul foamed over with health" (*BT,* "Attempt at a Self-Criticism," 4)—Nietzsche found a worldview in which the world of Becoming was affirmed and the conceptual pairs of "positive" and "negative" concepts were not ordered hierarchically. A Greek person in this culture, "having looked boldly into the terrible destructiveness of so-called world history as well as the cruelty of nature," was, "uniquely susceptible . . . to the tenderest and deepest suffering." But unlike Schopenhauer, who has seen and felt the same things, these Greeks did not submit to a "Buddhistic negation of the will" (*BT*, 7).[3] Nietzsche is impressed with these early Greeks because in their lives he finds "a formula for the highest affirmation, born of fullness, of overfullness, a Yes-saying without reservation, even to suffering, even to guilt, even to everything that is questionable and strange in existence" (*EH*, "The Birth of Tragedy," 2). These Greeks, Nietzsche applauds, found a way to affirm everything about the world of Becoming that the later "justifiers" and "improvers" found necessary to dispense with in their depiction of ultimate reality.

Silenus, the companion of Dionysus, has no good news when King Midas "asked him what was the best and most desirable thing of all for mankind" (*BT*, 3). He can say only:

> Oh, wretched ephemeral race, children of chance and misery, why do you compel me to tell you what it would be most expedient for you not to hear? What is best of all is utterly beyond your reach: not to be born, not to *be*, to be *nothing*. But the second best for you is—to die soon. (*BT*, 3)

These early Greeks were able to reverse the wisdom of Silenus. Nietzsche says of them, "to die soon is the worst of all for them, the next worst—to die at all" (*BT*, 3). They desired life.

They could reverse the wisdom of Silenus and affirm reality without denying its Dionysian aspects through art, in particular, "tragic art."

> Here, when the danger to his will is greatest, *art* approaches as a saving sorceress, expert at healing. She alone knows how to turn these nauseous thoughts about the horror or absurdity of existence into notions with which one can live. (*BT*, 7)

Tragic art can do this because it is, at one time, both Apollonian and Dionysian. "We must understand [pre-Euripidian] Greek tragedy as the Dionysian chorus which ever anew discharges itself in an Apollonian world of images" (*BT*, 8). It is Dionysian in the sense that it represents the terror and horror of existence. Pre-Euripidian tragedies were not tales of morality. Rather, they were truly tragic in the sense that the "good" and "just" were often destroyed. Greek tragedy is Apollonian insofar as these images of reality are delivered by Apollonian images. The horror of the primal void is rendered by "beautiful images of superior human lives."[4] The tragic drama presents us with beautiful, noble, and dignified individuals who maintain their dignity, nobility, and beauty even when faced with their destruction. By expressing the Dionysian truth of reality in Apollonian images, one is exposed to the great abyss of existence without being reduced to nihilistic despair. In tragic art, the terrible is transfigured into the sublime. John Sallis writes:

> Let it be said, then, that tragedy exposes one to the abyss, disclosing the abyss by way of a double mimesis; *and yet*, that tragedy, in its very disclosure of the abyss, protects, saves, even heals one from the destructive consequences that such exposure can have. . . . Exposing one mimetically to the abyss, tragedy at the same time lets the abyss be displaced, lets it be replaced with the sublime.[5]

Furthermore, because the Apollonian images are images of Dionysus, one is not presented with an overly optimistic and superficial view of reality.

Nietzsche was drawn to these early Greeks because he found them capable of living in the world with intensity, depth, and respect for the Dionysian nature of reality. They solved the problem of existence "aesthetically," not morally. What this means is that they did not interpret existence, with its vicissitudes and horrors, ethically or morally. Suffering is not justified because it is of some greater good for the universe. The universe is amoral and will not justify one's hope that all things turn out well. By "aesthetically," Nietzsche means, as Silk and Stern write, "if life is defensible at all, it can only be defended in the way that one creator might justify his handiwork to another: ethically unedifying, but marvelous to look at."[6] Thus one can affirm life in the world "*both* as a suffering individual *and* as part of a marvelous work of art."[7]

NIETZSCHE'S LATER
PROPOSAL FOR OVERCOMING NIHILISM

Nietzsche did, as is well known, eventually move away from his endorsement of the early Greek's ability to affirm life through tragic art. Part of his objection to what he had written was that these early Greeks were able to affirm the Dionysian truth about reality only when it was veiled by Apollo. Although he appreciated their more realistic approach, they still required a gloss or veil of sorts. For these Greeks, "art makes the sight of life bearable" (*HATH*, I:151). Their art

eased life. In this case, the tragic artists "soothe and heal only tem-
porarily, only for the moment" (*HATH*, I:148). When Nietzsche becomes more and more suspicious of all forms of "otherworldliness"
and "metaphysical consolations," as he does beginning with *Human,
All Too Human*, he cannot fail to notice such an escape going on in
The Birth of Tragedy. He accused himself of being an "art-deifier" (*BT*,
"Attempt at a Self-criticism," 7).

Starting with *Human, All Too Human*, Nietzsche seeks a more thoroughly "this-worldly" solution to the problem of nihilism. He wants to
"dispatch all metaphysical comforts to the devil" (*BT*, "Attempt at a
Self-criticism," 7). If reality is to be accepted in its entirety, one must
be able to look at its Dionysian core, the "deadly" truth of Becoming,
without squinting. What Nietzsche begins to realize is that after one
accepts the death of God and thinks it all the way through, one realizes that the "deadly" truth is not so deadly. The "sovereignty of Becoming" kills our sense of meaningfulness only when our criteria for
meaning are the categories of static Being.

When God dies and we vanquish all of God's shadows, this world,
the only world, achieves a new sense of innocence. There is no "True
World of Being" that differs from, and stands in judgment of, this
world. When Zarathustra first begins to think about the implications
of the death of God—namely, the reality of Becoming—he falls
"down as one dead" and remains lethargic for seven days (*Z*, III:13).
After this period, Zarathustra raises himself and, with a new sense of
the significance of God's death, eats an apple. Finding its "fragrance
lovely," Zarathustra rejoices in the newly de-deified world (*Z*, III:13).
The eating of the apple is a reversal of the original sin of Adam and
Eve. Creation has become innocent.[8] "The world," Zarathustra states,
"lies before me like a garden" (*Z*, III:13). By denying the existence of
God, we redeem the world (*TI*, "The Four Great Errors," 8).

The death of God opens a whole new set of liberating possibilities.
The situation is similar to what happens in *Zarathustra* when the lion
kills the great dragon in the chapter "The Three Metamorphosis." The
name of the dragon is "Thou Shalt," representing, as Peter Berkowitz
writes, "the symbol of mankind's duplicitous efforts to pass off artifi-
cial moral codes as the work of nature, God, or universal reason."[9] By
slaying the great dragon, the lion represents a victory over Christian-
slave morality. In *The Gay Science*, Nietzsche describes the liberating
potential of the death of God:

Indeed, we philosophers and "free spirits" feel, when we hear the news that the "old god is dead," as if a new dawn shone upon us; our heart overflows with gratitude, amazement, premonitions, expectation. At long last the horizon appears free to us again, even if it should not be bright; at long last our ships may venture out again, venture out to face any danger, all the daring of the lover of knowledge is permitted again; the sea, *our* sea, lies open again; perhaps there has never yet been such an "open sea." (*GS*, 343)

This situation is similar to what might have happened in Kafka's "Parable of the Law" if the man from the country came to realize that the Law did not exist. In this parable, a man leaves his home and family in search of the Law, which he thinks he must have. He finds the doorway to it, but it is blocked by a locked door and a guard. Thinking the Law is something he must have, he waits his entire lifetime in front of the door, hoping that it might someday open. For Nietzsche, the idea of a True World of Being functions in a manner similar to the Law. We take it as the mark of authentic reality but find it forever beyond our reach. Thus, we find this world lacking in possibilities. If the man from the country could have come to realize that there was no Law, he could have returned to the country. Similarly, when we realize that the True World of Being does not exist, we can return to this world, confident that it is the only world. The derogatory status of this world of Becoming falls away as the World of Being evaporates. "The true world—we have abolished. What world has remained? The apparent one perhaps? But no! *With the true world we have also abolished the apparent one*" (*TI*, "How the True World Finally Became a Fable," 6). By exposing the True World of Being and its accompanying table of "Thou Shalts" as fables, we are invited to a new appreciation of human life in its natural, worldly, and bodily setting. We can now "translate man back into nature; to become master over the many vain and overly enthusiastic interpretations and connotations" (*BGE*, 230). One no longer needs, as Zarathustra proclaims, "to bury one's head in the sand of heavenly things, but to bear it freely, an earthly head, which creates a meaning for the earth" (*Z*, I:3).

But we misconstrue Nietzsche if we think the ability to affirm life simply comes through the realization that we have regained our innocence and now stand in an open sea. To be sure, we have been shown the exit from a decadent, slavish, and oppressive interpretation of the human being and the world. This realization, though, is not sufficient to generate a sense of meaningfulness. It is only an invitation to give our life meaning. This realization is not meaning itself. The victory of the lion is only a transitional stage.

The death of God involves much more than the demise of any single system of values. One of the fundamental aspects of the death of God is that values are not inscribed in the fabric of reality; they are not simply given. "Whatever has *value* in our world now does not have value in itself, according to its nature—nature is always valueless, but has been *given* value at some time, as a present" (*GS*, 301). After the death of God, meaning is not simply there to be had. For Nietzsche, giving life value requires that we become creators and create our own values. "Can you give yourself your own evil and your own good and hang your own will over yourself as a law?" (*Z*, I:17) If we can, we will overcome the sense of futility imparted by the death of God. "Creation—that is the great redemption from suffering and life's growing light" (*Z*, II:2).

So what sort of meaning should we give? Surely Nietzsche cannot endorse all such possibilities. If so, where would the force of his criticism of Christianity and the other improvement moralities be rooted? But Nietzsche does not, at least explicitly, offer much advice in terms of content. To be sure, the person who states "one repays a teacher badly if one always remains nothing but a pupil" (*Z*, I:2) must remain somewhat silent on these matters. We must lose Zarathustra and find ourselves (*Z*, I:22).[10]

In spite of this silence, however, Nietzsche does give us some criteria by which we might adjudicate the meanings and paths we choose. The first, as we saw in the previous chapter, is that it ought to heighten our feeling of power and give us a sense of reverence for ourselves. Nietzsche criticizes improvement-morality because it attempts to improve humanity through a denial of the right to be an individual with needs, desires, instincts, and self-interests. Nietzsche wants a worldview that allows these rights. We are entitled to seek ourselves in the world. Also, we must, as Zarathustra teaches, "*remain faithful to the earth*," and we should not believe those "who speak . . . of otherworldly hopes" (*Z*, I:3)! Whatever meaning we give should be a worldly and natural one. It should be one in which it is life in *this* world that is meaningful.

A second and more provocative criterion is Nietzsche's doctrine of eternal return. How would you feel, Nietzsche asks, if a demon were to come to you with the following proposal:

This life as you now live it and have lived it, you will have to live once more and innumerable times more; and there will be nothing new in it, but every pain and every joy and every thought and sigh and everything unutterably small or great in your life will have to return to you, all in the same succession and sequence—even this spider and this moonlight between the trees, and even this moment and I myself. The eternal hourglass of existence is turned upside down again and again, and you with it, speck of dust. (*GS*, 341)

Would we curse the demon, or would we embrace him and welcome the opportunity to live our lives again, again, and again, with no detail omitted? Affirming worldly life requires that we live in such a way that we could say yes to the demon, transforming the cosmic nihilism of a purposeless world into a divine way of thinking. Nietzsche thinks saying yes to the demon is a sign that we have lived life in such a way that its meaning is intrinsic to the life itself. The doctrine of eternal return is the "highest formula for affirmation that is at all attainable" (*EH*, "Thus Spoke Zarathustra," 1).

In the remainder of this chapter, I would like to discuss what sort of lives Nietzsche himself admired and thought potentially capable of saying yes to the demon. I discuss "the child," Goethe, Nietzsche himself, and the *Übermensch*. In each of these examples, there is a particular attitude that exemplifies an affirmative stance toward life in a godless world.

The Child and the Life of Playful Creativity

A man's maturity—consists in having found again the seriousness one had as a child at play.

—*Nietzsche*, Beyond Good and Evil

One of Nietzsche's "Yes-sayers" is the child in "Thus Spoke Zarathustra" who appears after the lion kills the great dragon. In this newly opened space, one can become childlike, enjoying and embodying the innocence of Becoming, living affirmatively. "The child is innocence and forgetting, a new beginning, a game, a self-propelled wheel, a first movement, a sacred 'Yes.' For the game of creation, my brothers, a sacred 'Yes' is needed" (*Z*, I:1). What Nietzsche admires about the child is its naturalness and sense of creative play. This naturalness is displayed in the fact that a child often does not differentiate itself from its world. Its inner reality is largely synonymous with its outer life. The child *is* its activity. The child is not forever questioning its authenticity and wondering whether its actions are morally correct. The child does not, as did Pascal, continually adjudicate its behavior and feelings on the basis of the "moral world order." The child has not lost its natural spontaneity and does not suffer from the "bad conscience" so evident in the Christian. As Joan Stambaugh writes, the child, for Nietzsche, is transparent to the world.[11]

The Yes-saying of the child is evident in the fact that its primary mode of being in the world is *play*. The child's way of life is like that of a game that has no purpose other than the playing of the game, with the act of playing being itself the meaning of the game. The child is not burdened with a heavy sense of responsibility and does not have to figure anything out. One of Nietzsche's objections to Socrates was that Socrates made the purpose of existence in this world the procurement of a "philosophical nature" that would allow one to separate "truth" from appearance. This philosophical nature eventually would deliver one out of the delusional world of Becoming, with its unstable and corrupt particulars. Achieving authenticity, for Nietzsche's Socrates, depended on being able to see beyond the world of fraudulent Becoming and appearance. In a world of purposeless Becoming that is not judged inferior by a Transcendent True World of Being, one can live like a child, enjoying this world, caring little whether one's games and fantasies are completely devoid of illusion. Unlike Socrates' "theoretical man," who must live bound to the notion that static, ahistorical truth is necessary, Nietzsche's child is free to play in, experiment with, and explore this world of appearance. One does not need to live a life that is forever responsible for looking beneath the surface.

For Nietzsche, the sort of truth that Socrates seeks does not exist. The world of Becoming is the only world. We have no right to the idea that some greater, more perfect world exists. There is no static True World of Being. "What is required . . . is to stop courageously at the surface, the fold, the skin, to adore appearance, to believe in forms, tones, words, in the whole Olympus of appearance" (*GS*, preface, 4).

Nietzsche's denial of the True World of Being should not be mistaken, as I said earlier, with the idea that Nietzsche denied that there is a way in which the world really is. Reality is Becoming, which he later comes to articulate by saying reality is the will to power (*BGE*, 36). The world is a "monster of energy," which is eternally "self-creating and self-destroying" (*WP*, 1067; 1885). Although Nietzsche often denied he was doing metaphysics, we need to understand this statement as only the denial of a particular type of metaphysics—namely, Platonism. Nietzsche was opposed to metaphysics when the *meta-* was taken as referring to "above." Nietzsche *is* a metaphysician, however, in the sense that he is offering an account of reality as it is. Here, the *meta-* refers to "comprehensive."[12]

One of the more important consequences of Nietzsche's cosmology is that human beings are set free from claims to truth that purport dogmatic certainty (other than the truth that reality is Becoming). If reality is Becoming, then it has a richness that defies simple and univocal analysis.[13] Reality is, in this way, "ambiguous." There is no simple scheme of interpretation, therefore, that can be said to exhaust its reality. The world has become, Nietzsche says, "'infinite' for us all over again, inasmuch as we cannot reject the possibility that *it may include infinite interpretations*" (*GS*, 374). This possibility of infinite interpretations allows a playful, experimental, and creative approach to life in the world. It gives us a dimension of freedom for how we want to live.[14] We can shape reality.[15]

In Nietzsche's innocent world of Becoming, we are not locked within any single interpretation of reality that purports that reality is static. Rather, we are released into a labyrinth where we can find happiness. "The most spiritual men, as the strongest, find their happiness where others would find their destruction: in the labyrinth" (*A*, 57). The happiness that one finds is the happiness of a playful and aesthetic life of shaping reality. By becoming more childlike (which does not mean more childish), we can learn to live a life of art.

Goethe and the Love of Fate

Another one of Nietzsche's "Yes-sayers" is Goethe. He saw Goethe as a kindred spirit, united with him in his attack on Christianity. "Goethe is the last German for whom I have any reverence" (*TI*, "Skirmishes of an Untimely Man," 51). One of the things Nietzsche admired about Goethe was that he, like the child, lived the life of the artist. To Nietzsche, as Walter Kaufmann writes, Goethe represented the "hardness of the creator who creates himself."[16] More important, Goethe's artistic impulse stems from a feeling of overfullness, richness, and gratitude. He is, in this way, similar to Zarathustra, who feels like a "cup that wants to overflow" (*Z*, prologue, 1). This puts Goethe in contrast to the tradition of romanticism, which Nietzsche thinks suffers from an "impoverishment of life" (*GS*, 370).

Nietzsche also admires Goethe for his trusting attitude toward fate. Describing Goethe's attitude, Nietzsche writes, "Such a spirit who has *become free* stands amid the cosmos with a joyous and trusting fatalism" (*TI*, "Skirmishes of an Untimely Man," 49). Goethe can stand amid the cosmos with a sense of joy and trust because he accepts its innocence. Unlike the nihilistic improvers, Goethe does not consider this world to be in the wrong. With this attitude, Goethe embodies one of Nietzsche's formulas for greatness in a human being, *amor fati*, which he describes with the following:

> That one wants nothing to be different, not forward, not backward, not in all eternity. Not merely bear what is necessary, still less conceal it— all idealism is mendaciousness in the face of what is necessary—but *love* it. (*EH*, "Why I Am So Clever," 10)

In his trusting attitude, Goethe is free from both *ressentiment* and the feeling that life is merely a road to something greater. He does not need hope as a justification for the present.[17]

It needs to be understood that Nietzsche's conception of *amor fati* is not a passive fatalism. It is not fatalism as traditionally understood. The traditional fatalist resents the passage of time, accepting it, merely enduring it as something that one is powerless against. In contrast, for Nietzsche, as Thiele writes, "the lover of fate . . . makes everything that comes his way a cause for celebration."[18] Above all, *amor fati* represents a freedom from *ressentiment* and an affirmation of reality as it is.

To achieve *amor fati,* one must take a new attitude toward the passage of time. A culture of decadence and nihilism displays a resentful attitude toward the passage of time. Time destroys human achievements and gives a sickening feeling of "it was." "'It was'—that is the name of the will's gnashing of teeth and most secret melancholy" (*Z*, II:20). This feeling is what leads to the desire to escape the passage of time. "Alas," preaches one who suffers from the passage of time, "where is redemption from the flux of things and from the punishment called existence?" (*Z*, II:20). Overcoming this melancholic feeling toward the incessant passage of time requires, Nietzsche thinks, the transformation of the feeling "it was" to "thus I willed it" (*Z*, II:20). "All 'it was' is a fragment, a riddle, a dreadful accident—until the creative will says to it, 'But thus I willed it.' Until the creative will says to it, 'But thus I will it; thus I shall will it" (*Z*, II:20). If we can love our fate by embracing everything as if it were our own choice, we are in a prime position to be able to say yes to the prospect of eternal return. Nietzsche describes what he takes to be the ideal human being:

> The ideal of the most high-spirited, alive, and world-affirming human being who has not only come to terms and learned to get along with whatever was and is, but who wants to have *what was and is* repeated into all eternity, shouting insatiably *da capo*. (*BGE*, 56)

Nietzsche and the Affirmation of Suffering

> Gradually it has become clear to me what every great philosophy so far has been: namely, the personal confession of its author and a kind of involuntary and unconscious memoir.
>
> —*Nietzsche*, Beyond Good and Evil

> Who will sing a song for us, a morning song, so sunny, so light, so fledged that it will not chase the blues away but invite them instead to join in the singing and dancing?
>
> —*Nietzsche*, The Gay Science

If, as Nietzsche says, philosophy is autobiography, we will do well to look at his own life as an example of one who says yes to the demon who introduces the idea of eternal return. At the end of his forty-fourth year—"a perfect day when everything is ripening and not only grapes turn brown"—Nietzsche asked, "*How could I fail to be grateful to my whole life*" (*EH*, interstice)?[19] Nietzsche's gratitude is not a simple thankfulness for a charmed and easy life. It is gratitude for a life plagued by incessant ill health, long periods of loneliness, feelings of homelessness, unrequited love, an overly doting mother and sister, and other misfortunes. We might, therefore, admire Nietzsche's proclamation of gratitude as all the more remarkable given that he can say yes *in spite of* all these obstacles. But we would be wrong to phrase it this way. Nietzsche clearly claims that his gratitude, his claim that his "life is simply wonderful" (*EH*, "Why I Am So Clever," 9), is not *in spite of* his distress. An "in-spite-of affirmation" is one tinged with *ressentiment*, with the feeling that life could and should have been otherwise. Rather, Nietzsche affirms his life and the prospect of eternal return *within* all of its distress.

> You see that I do not want to take leave ungratefully from that time of severe sickness whose profits I have not yet exhausted even today. I am very conscious of the advantages that my fickle health gives me over all robust squares. (*GS*, preface, 3)

Throughout the preface of *The Gay Science*, Nietzsche writes about issues concerning the relationship between health and sickness. It is a book written, he states, after a period of the "tyranny of pain" (*GS*, preface, 1). But, throughout this tyranny, Nietzsche was able to refuse the *"conclusion* of pain" (*GS*, preface, 1). By "conclusion of pain," Nietzsche is referring to the Christian-moral interpretation of distress, with its hierarchical dualism that sees suffering as an argument against existence. As we saw, for Nietzsche, pain, distress, and the other "negative" qualities are as real as their opposites. They cannot simply be eliminated. "Yet," Nietzsche writes, "one should not jump to the conclusion that this necessarily makes one gloomy. Even love of life is still possible" (*GS*, preface, 3). How, then, did Nietzsche think this love and affirmation were possible? In the first place, Nietzsche can affirm distress and its various manifestations because he sees them as leading to a greater appreciation of health and well-being.

> In the end, lest what is most important remain unsaid: from such abysses, from such severe sickness, also from the sickness of severe suspicion, one returns *newborn*, having shed one's skin, more ticklish and malicious, with a more delicate taste for joy, with a tenderer tongue for all things, with merrier senses, with a second dangerous innocence in joy, more child-like and yet a hundred times subtler than one has ever been before. (*GS*, preface, 4)

Here Nietzsche is endorsing the idea that sickness and distress provide one with a perspective by which one can better appreciate periods of health. After sickness, everything appears new and fresh again. "Only where there are tombs," says Zarathustra, "are there resurrections" (*Z*, II:11).

This attitude towards distress is not entirely affirmative, however. These periods are merely endured. This is the attitude of the "Russian fatalist," who, "finding a campaign too strenuous finally lies down in the snow" (*EH*, "Why I Am So Wise," 6). This sort of fatalism—which is different than that of *amor fati*—can preserve life by inducing a state of hibernation in which one can refuse the conclusion of pain by sleeping through it. But in *Thus Spoke Zarathustra*, Nietzsche develops a view that attempts to affirm the actual contents of moments of distress. He writes, "Have you ever said Yes to a single joy? O my friends, then you said Yes too to *all* woe. All things are entangled, ensnared, enamored" (*Z*, IV:19). In this passage, we find the idea that all moments have a history and are intimately connected to their predecessors. Remove one thing from the past and the entirety of what is to come will be altered. Therefore, all moments of deep happiness and joy are the offspring of everything that has come before, including all moments of distress. "If you ever wanted one thing twice, if ever you said, 'You please me, happiness! Abide, moment!' then you wanted *all* back" (*Z*, IV:19). A life composed of periods of distress can be affirmed if one has achieved moments of profound happiness.

When one realizes that all moments are connected to their pasts, one could desire their return. In fact, a frequent occurrence is someone who claims that the diagnosis of a terminal disease has, in a sense, awakened them from a slumber, inviting them to a new appreciation of life. There is a joke that states that the perfect gift for the person who has everything is cancer. One might then attribute one's happiness to the illness, thus affirming it as necessary.

Nietzsche also found it possible to affirm his life of suffering because he felt that experiences of distress made one more profound.

Only great pain, the long, slow pain that takes its time—on which we are burned, as it were with green wood—compels us philosophers to descend into our ultimate depths and to put aside all trust, everything good-natured, everything that would interpose a veil, that is mild, that is medium—things in which formerly we may have found our humanity. (*GS*, preface, 3)

These comments should be seen in relation to Nietzsche's criticism of the desire for comfort. Nietzsche thinks that one achieves comfort only by the removal of tensions, which results in a sort of anesthesia. The experience of pain and suffering can increase profundity insofar as they increase the degree of tension in experience. The willingness to feel pain without repressing it adds complexity to experience. In a passage worth quoting at length, Nietzsche writes:

Anyone who manages to experience the history of humanity as a whole as *his own history* will feel in an enormously generalized way all the

grief of an invalid who thinks of health, of an old man who thinks of the
dreams of his youth, of a lover deprived of his beloved, of the martyr
whose ideal is perishing, of the hero on the evening after a battle that
has decided nothing but brought him wounds and the loss of his friend.
But if one endured, if one *could* endure this immense sum of grief of all
kinds while yet being the hero who, as the second day of battle breaks,
welcomes the dawn and his fortune . . if one could finally contain all this
in one soul and crown it into a single feeling—this would surely have to
result in a happiness that humanity has not yet known so far: the happiness of a god full of power and life, full of tears and laughter. . . . This
godlike feeling would then be called—humanness. (*GS*, 337)

In this passage, Nietzsche is suggesting that if one can experience the
suffering that is indigenous to life in the world of Becoming without
taking it as an argument against existence, one will be opened to a
whole new set of experiences never before known. One may accomplish "a depth of happiness in which even what is most painful and
gloomy does not seem something opposite but rather conditioned,
provoked, a *necessary* color in such a superabundance of light" (*EH*,
"Thus Spoke Zarathustra," 3).

The *Übermensch*

The greater part of what my neighbors call good I believe in my soul
to be bad, and if I repent of anything, it is very likely to be my good
behavior.

—*Henry David Thoreau*, Walden, or Life in the Woods

Although it is often said that the *Übermensch* is Nietzsche's dominant
conception of the ideal human being,[20] Nietzsche's description of this
concept is, as Bernd Magnus writes, "very slim."[21] But Nietzsche does
give enough of a picture to allow us to discover one more quality or
attitude that Nietzsche thinks to be exemplary of one who affirms
worldly life. The feature I want to highlight is what can be called the
Übermensch's "inner economy." What I mean by this term concerns
the manner in which the instincts, drives, and passions are regulated
and managed.

Much of Nietzsche's argument against both improvement and
slave morality has to do with the way in which they denigrated humanity's instinctual and bodily life. In these moralities the approach
is toward the "taming" of the bodily life through extirpation.

Socrates advocated "rationality at any price." Christianity continued this denigration of bodily life, as did Kant with his disinterested aesthetic and categorical imperative. In all of these cases authentic living had very little to do with bodily life or self-interest. The development of this trend is one of the major contributing factors to the apathy of the "last man" who no longer has any desire to do anything of much consequence because all possibilities have been vitiated. The *Übermensch* is the antithesis of the last man. Whereas the last man is the outcome of slave morality, the morality of the *Übermensch* bears a close resemblance to master morality.[22] Nietzsche admires master morality because of its self-centeredness, sense of power, reverence for nobility, respect for the body, and, above all, naturalness.

I mentioned previously that Nietzsche's dispute with improvement-morality did not mean he thought human beings were perfectly formed in their natural state. At the core, for Nietzsche, human beings are a manifold of passions, conflicting drives and instincts. "In man there is material, fragment, excess, clay, dirt, nonsense, chaos" (*BGE*, 225). Nietzsche calls this the creaturely aspect of human nature. But human beings also have the ability to control this manifold; they are also creators. "In man there is also creator, formgiver, hammer hardness, spectator divinity, and seventh day" (*BGE*, 225). Therefore, Nietzsche's call to renaturalize our concept of human nature should not be understood as a call to return to a beastly state. The creature within must be overcome. Nietzsche's return to nature should be, as he says, understood as an "ascent." "I too speak of a 'return to nature,' although it is really not a going back but an *ascent*" (*TI*, "Skirmishes of an Untimely Man," 48).

It is the *Übermensch* who ascends to a higher state of being by forming something out of the given and chaotic creature. The *Übermensch* orders the conflicting drives and instincts so that they can be sublimated into a single purpose. This approach is fundamentally different from the approach to the "anarchy of the instincts" found in Socrates. Socrates attempted merely to tame them, whereas Nietzsche's *Übermensch* unifies and channels them. When faced with conflicting drives and instincts, the Socratic-theoretical individual deals with this discord through elimination. In the *Übermensch* the instincts still speak. "The 'great man' is great owing to the free play and scope of his desires and to the yet greater power that knows how to press these magnificent monsters into service" (*WP*, 933; 1887).

Furthermore, Nietzsche thinks the more "affects" one allows to speak, the richer the possible outcome.

The highest man would have the greatest multiplicity of drives, in the relatively greatest strength that can be endured. Indeed, where the plant "man" shows himself strongest one finds instincts that conflict power-fully (e.g., in Shakespeare), but are controlled. (*WP*, 966; 1884)

In the same way that the inclusion of suffering within experience (as opposed to a mere repression) leads to experiences with greater complexity, depth, and profundity, the *Übermensch* presses the conflicting drives into a unity that is all the greater because of its contained and coherent diversity. Like Zarathustra, in the *Übermensch* "all opposites are blended into a new unity" (*EH*, "Thus Spoke Zarathustra," 6). The *Übermensch* listens to the body but is in control of it. Because of this control, the *Übermensch* can harness the instincts and drives for great things. As Schacht writes, the *Übermensch* represents "a transformation of life beyond the healthy and robust but insipid animality, and also beyond that of sickened and weakened . . . all-too-human humanity."[23]

For Nietzsche, the death of God and the revealed purposeless universe are facts. But the threat that human life in the world is now meaningless can be overcome. In fact, it is precisely the death of God that makes it possible for humanity to come to a new appreciation and affirmation of life in the world of Becoming.

NOTES

1. David Farrell Krell, *Infectious Nietzsche* (Bloomington: Indiana University Press, 1996), 57.

2. Tyler Roberts, *Contesting Spirit: Nietzsche, Affirmation, Religion* (Princeton, N.J.: Princeton University Press, 1998), 155–56.

3. Although the intellectual scene in nineteenth-century Germany exhibited a great interest in Asian thought, it did not, as a whole, possess an accurate understanding of it. For an account of Nietzsche's background in Asian thought, see Johann Figl's "Nietzsche's Early Encounter with Asian Thought," in *Nietzsche and Asian Thought*, ed. Graham Parkes (Chicago: University of Chicago Press, 1991), 51–63.

4. Hayden White, *Metahistory: The Historical Imagination in Nineteenth-Century Europe* (Baltimore: Johns Hopkins University Press, 1973), 338.

5. John Sallis, *Nietzsche and the Space of Tragedy* (Chicago: University of Chicago Press, 1991), 93.

6. M. S. Silk and J. P. Stern, *Nietzsche on Tragedy* (Cambridge: Cambridge University Press, 1981), 295.

7. Silk and Stern, *Nietzsche on Tragedy*, 295.

8. Brian Ingraffia, *Postmodern Theory and Biblical Theology* (Cambridge: Cambridge University Press, 1995), 95.

9. Peter Berkowitz, *Nietzsche: The Ethics of an Immoralist* (Cambridge, Mass.: Harvard University Press, 1995), 181.

10. In a letter made famous by Heidegger, Nietzsche tells Georg Brandes, "Once you discovered me, it was no great feat to find me: the difficulty now is to lose me." Nietzsche to Georg Brandes, 4 January 1889, Turin, *Selected Letters of Friedrich Nietzsche*, trans. and ed. Christopher Middleton (Chicago: University of Chicago Press, 1969), 345.

11. Joan Stambaugh, *The Other Nietzsche* (Albany: State University of New York Press, 1994), 112.

12. Although Richard Schacht is uncomfortable with calling Nietzsche's philosophy "metaphysical," he does use the term "non-metaphysical cosmology" as a description of what Nietzsche is doing. See *Nietzsche* (London: Routledge, 1992), 204.

13. Schacht, *Nietzsche*, 203.

14. Stambaugh, *The Other Nietzsche*, 126.

15. Nietzsche is not saying that it is just as easy to change your views as it is to change your clothes. However, such changes are possible and desirable.

16. Walter Kaufmann, *Nietzsche*, 4th ed. (Princeton, N.J.: Princeton University Press, 1974), 155.

17. Leslie Thiele quotes Goethe: "Hope is the second soul of unhappiness." *Friedrich Nietzsche and the Politics of the Soul: A Study of Heroic Individualism* (Princeton. N.J.: Princeton University Press, 1990), 201.

18. Thiele, *Friedrich Nietzsche and the Politics of the Soul*, 199.

19. This page appears between the preface and the first chapter and has no page number or title.

20. Thiele, *Friedrich Nietzsche and the Politics of the Soul*, 184.

21. Bernd Magnus, *Nietzsche's Existential Imperative* (Bloomington: Indiana University Press, 1978), 32.

22. Magnus, *Nietzsche's Existential Imperative*, 33.

23. Schacht, *Nietzsche*, 394.

6

Whitehead's Criticism of the Classical Christian Doctrine of God

In this chapter, I turn my attention to Whitehead's criticism of the classical doctrine of God. Whitehead was critical of a number of aspects of this doctrine, but for the most part, these aspects are connected to the presupposition that God is, and must be, immutable. Thus, in manner similar to Nietzsche, Whitehead is wary of the prejudice toward the idea that static Being is the prime characteristic of eminent reality.

Whitehead was interested in several facets of religion. As a philosopher, much of his interest was in the idea of God as a necessary part of his own metaphysics. He was also interested in the history of religion and comparative religion, and these aspects were not unrelated for him. The need for a suitable doctrine of God required Whitehead to sort through previous ideas of God that have appeared throughout history and among the various world religions. We will have the opportunity to discuss both of these aspects. In this chapter, I consider Whitehead's views of the history of Christian theology, especially the classical conception of God, of which he was critical for both philosophical and ethical reasons.

THE RELIGIOUS PROBLEM

In our discussion of Nietzsche, we saw that one of the fundamental problems facing human beings is whether human existence is ultimately meaningful given the apparent fact that we live in a finite world wrought with change. Finitude and transience, it is thought, present a threat to the possible meaningfulness of human existence. This threat is derived from the presupposition that meaningfulness is often associated with that which is permanent. Remember that according to Nietzsche, the primary answer to the threat of meaningfulness in the Western tradition has been to assert that there is a metaphysical realm that is eternal and devoid of change. Furthermore, Nietzsche states that Christianity claims that the problem of finitude and the ensuing threat to meaningfulness can be overcome by a faith that one will ultimately be delivered to this metaphysical realm of the True World of Being. Much of Nietzsche's criticism stems from Christianity's otherworldliness. Thus, one aspect of the problem with the Christian worldview is its ontological dualism, which construes the True World of Being as simply and statically permanent and finds the world in which we live, the apparent world, to be simply transient and finite. Ethical problems arise, Nietzsche thinks, within this cosmology because it does not enable one to find any intrinsic meaning and value to life in this finite world.

In his analysis of religion, Whitehead understands religion as focused on a similar problem. For Whitehead, the central problem of human existence that religion attempts to answer stems from a paradox. The paradox is that human beings, on the one hand, desire novelty and, yet on the other hand, are "haunted by terror at the loss of the past, with its familiarities and loved ones" (*PR*, 340). Human beings desire novelty but realize that novelty requires transition and loss. Thus, the problem is whether it is possible to achieve novelty without the loss of values achieved in the past. "The most general formulation of the religious problem is the question whether the process of the temporal world passes into the formation of other actualities, bound together in an order in which novelty does not mean loss" (*PR*, 340). In other words, the problem faced by religion is simply whether the transience and finitude of human existence comprise the whole story.

One of the fundamental differences between Nietzsche and Whitehead is that Whitehead puts forward a doctrine of God that allows one to answer no to the question of whether transience is the whole story. As I discuss in chapter 8, Whitehead holds that the values achieved in the temporal world are retained everlastingly in God's "consequent nature." Although "process entails loss," Whitehead writes, "there is no reason, on any metaphysical generality, why this should be the whole story" (*PR*, 340). Without such optimism, "human life," Whitehead writes, "is a flash of occasional enjoyments lighting up a mass of pain and misery, a bagatelle of transient experience" (*SMW*, 192). On the surface, Whitehead's desire for this sort of solution to the problem of finitude puts him at odds with Nietzsche's argument that any such solution is a form of decadence. But, as I later argue, the manner in which Whitehead accomplishes this solution avoids most of the problems Nietzsche described. For the moment, I would like to point out that Whitehead's use of God to solve the problem of finitude does not imply that, in the end, what one achieves through religious faith is some sort of anesthetic comfort. Rather, as Whitehead writes, "the worship of God is not a rule of safety," nor does it entail the "repression of the high hope of adventure" (*SMW*, 192).

For Nietzsche, transcendental solutions to the problem of existence are decadent because they imply that flux, becoming, fluidity, suffering, and finitude are things undesirable in principle. The permanence sought by decadent religion and philosophy is a permanence completely devoid of the categories of Becoming. The conceptual logic governing the decadent solution is that opposing concepts are not interrelated but irreconcilably dualistic. One seeks absolute permanence, thus desiring a complete and absolute escape from fluidity and becoming. Whitehead shares Nietzsche's conviction that this sort of conceptual logic is extremely problematic, especially in the area of religious discourse. In fact, I would like to suggest that when Whitehead criticizes theological doctrines, it is often because they imply this sort of logic, and the problem with the logic is that it is all too simplistic. For Whitehead, the chief danger to philosophical discourse "is narrowness in the selection of the evidence" (*PR*, 337). This danger is at its peak when one is considering "ultimate ideals," which are fashioned around the two notions of permanence and flux, usually stressing one or the other (*PR*, 338). The great danger is that when considering contrasting ideals, one will opt for one ideal at the expense of the contrasting ideal on the basis of a too narrow selection of evidence. For example, when comparing the "stern self-restraint of Roman farmers in the early history of the [Roman] republic" with "the aesthetic culture of Ancient Greece" or the "Augustan epoch in Rome," it is a sign of "blindness" to view one or the other with sheer contempt. Blindness ensues when one views reality solely through the lens of *either* permanence and conservative ideals *or* fluidity and more carefree tendencies. The capacity to see greatness in each of the ideals requires that we take a larger view of the nature of reality, understanding that it is, in some way, both permanent and fluid, thus having a place for both ideals. "In the inescapable flux, there is something that abides; in the overwhelming permanence, there is an element that escapes into flux. . . . Those who would disjoin the two elements can find no interpretation of patent facts" (*PR*, 338).

PROBLEMS WITH THE CLASSICAL DOCTRINE OF GOD

Theological discourse, especially in regard to the nature of God, has been especially prone to committing the error of narrowness in the selection of evidence, putting forth one-sided views that, Hartshorne writes, "seek to distinguish God from all else by putting God on one side of a long list of contraries" and the world on the other.[1] In his writings, Whitehead's principal argument against the traditional doctrine of God is philosophical: the categories that have been used to define and describe the nature of God are different from the ones used to describe the nature of this world. In other words, God has been paid false "metaphysical compliments" (*SMW*, 179). God has long been characterized as possessing a host of "positive" concepts—such as absolute, infinite, necessary, eternal, free, and independent—whereas the world has been given the opposite qualities: relative, finite, contingent, temporal, determined, and dependent. These compliments provide the basis for a supernaturalistic theology. Here, God is thought to be the free creator of the laws of nature and is, in no way whatsoever, subject to these laws. God transcends the world and is qualitatively different from it. This situation is undesirable because it does not allow one to put forward a "one substance cosmology," by which all actual entities are characterized by the same metaphysical principles.

Aware of the innumerable difficulties of ontological dualisms, Whitehead sought a cosmology by which *all* entities are characterized by the same metaphysical principles, including God. "In the philosophy of organism, as developed here, God's existence is not generically different from that of other actual entities" (*PR*, 75).[2] When God is paid metaphysical compliments, one can use the concept to explain anything with no regard to reason or coherence. Whatever is difficult to understand or explain can be attributed to God as a *deus ex machina*. Whitehead lists Berkeley and Leibniz as guilty of this act (*SMW*, 156). We must avoid, Whitehead says, "the easy assumption that there is an ultimate reality which, in some unexplained way, is to be appealed to for the removal of perplexity" (*SMW*, 92).

One of the (false) compliments paid to God was to exempt God from the seemingly ugly business of change, becoming, relativity, and the like. The compliment seemed necessary because most early Christian theologians were working with the axiom inherited from Platonism and neo-Platonism that eminent reality is static. "The static absolute has been passed over to philosophic theology, as a primary presupposition" (*MT*, 81). For God to be a God worthy of worship, God must surely be perfect. And since perfection was equated with the absence of any change whatsoever, God must be statically and absolutely permanent.

The Platonic Heritage of Christian Theology

At this point, it is necessary to look at certain aspects of Whitehead's assessment of Platonism, especially as they pertain to the notion of a static absolute. This discussion will show that aspects of Whitehead's criticism of Plato have much in common with Nietzsche's criticism of Socrates. But before proceeding, it must be stressed that what follows is by no means Whitehead's entire assessment of Plato's thought. In fact, it is grossly one-sided. Most of Whitehead's comments regarding Plato's contributions to Western thought are highly favorable. This twofold assessment of Platonism is not the result of careless thinking on Whitehead's part. Rather, it is due to the fact that both the positive strand and negative strand can be found in Plato's many writings. As Whitehead states, Plato was a great metaphysician, but not a good systematizer (*AI*, 166). For example, Plato wavered inconsistently between two different conceptions of divine agency. In the first case, which Whitehead praises and makes great use of, is the idea that "the divine element is to be conceived as a persuasive agency" (*AI*, 166). But, in the second case, divine agency is conceived as "the Supreme agency of compulsion" (*AI*, 166).

Platonism, Whitehead thinks, is one of the parties responsible for infecting Western thought with the "static fallacy," which is the belief that change is accidental and that static permanence is ultimately real. In contrast, Whitehead writes, "There is no halt in which the actuality is just its static self, accidentally played upon by qualifications derived from the shift of circumstances" (*AI*, 274–75). Plato committed this fallacy because he was "deceived by the beauty of mathematics" (*AI*, 275). He assumed that mathematics dealt with entities that "introduced no sense either of transition or of creation" (*MT*, 80).[3] As such, mathematics appeared to offer dazzling and impressive "glimpses of eternity" (*MT*, 81). With these glimpses, Whitehead continues, Plato went on to conceive "ultimate reality in the guise of static existences with timeless interrelations. *Perfection was unrelated to transition.* Creation, with its world in change, was an inferior avocation of a static absolute" (*MT*, 81; emphasis added). This is Plato's "super-world of ideas, forever perfect and forever interwoven" (*AI*, 275). Most important, it is a world presumed to be perfect because it admits no change, decay, or transition. Its constituents are just and always themselves. "In this imagined realm there is no passage, no loss, no gain. It is complete in itself. . . . It is therefore the realm of the 'completely real'" (*MT*, 68).

One of the problems with Plato's cosmology is that it construes *permanence* and *fluidity* as antithetical concepts, incapable of inhering together within any single actual entity. Within this conceptual system, the only status that can be given to the world of change is that of illusion. Any other description would involve one in a terrible contradiction.

> If the opposites, static and fluent, have once been so explained as separately to characterize diverse actualities, the interplay between the thing which is static and the things which are fluent involves contradiction at every step in its explanation. *Such philosophies must include the notion of "illusion" as a fundamental principle—the notion of "mere appearance."* This is the final Platonic problem. (*PR*, 346–47; emphasis added)

Under the influence of mathematics, Plato turns our attention away from the world of change, upward toward a timeless realm of static entities presumed to be perfect and eminently real by means of their lack of transition. The world of change is "real" only insofar as it imitates these forms. It is composed of only "second-rate substitutes and never the originals" (*AI*, 168). Because the forms are not incarnated in the particulars but only imitated by the particulars, the particulars retain the status of mere appearance. Similarly to Nietzsche, Whitehead is opposed to a realm of static permanence that is presumed to be eminently real. Such an understanding must always involve the denigration of the world in which we live to the level of mere appearance.

Along with issuing this statement about the lack of value inherent in the world of change, Plato's dualistic cosmology, with its eternally perfect realm of static and unchanging forms, leads Whitehead to another concern similar to Nietzsche's claim that Socratic philosophy is decadent and produces further decadence. For Nietzsche, "decadence" refers to those individuals, societies, and systems of thought that exhibit a certain weariness for life in the world and all that it includes. Socrates is decadent because he seeks an escape from the world of Becoming into a realm where Dionysus has been denied admission. Socrates yearns for a wholly Apollonian reality where everything is simply and eternally what it is. This desire, says Nietzsche, requires one to withdraw from, and forsake, life in the world. The flight to a world perfect in virtue of its changelessness and lack of suffering is a major contributing factor to the life of the comfortable, but tensionless, "last man."

Whitehead continues this line of thought, writing that Plato's endorsement of a realm of static perfection and its dismissal of turmoil is "the outcome of tired decadence" (*MT*, 80). Whitehead is using "decadence" in a manner similar to Nietzsche. In *Adventures of Ideas*, he writes, "The prolongation of outworn forms of life means a slow decadence in which there is a repetition without any fruit in the reaping of value" (*AI*, 78). Life is in decline when past forms are merely repeated. Decadence refers to a refusal towards change and growth. A "decadent habit of mind" is one that looks to the past only with the desire to repeat it (*AI*, 273). It is the preference for the static maintenance of perfection and is associated with otherworldliness (*AI*, 81). In *The Function of Reason*, Whitehead defines fatigue along the lines of decadence. "Fatigue means the operation of excluding the impulse towards novelty" (*FR*, 23). Plato's world of eminently real Forms is the outcome of decadence because it bars the turmoil of transition from its scheme.

Whereas Plato seems to suppose that it would be possible to enjoy some perfection eternally, Whitehead would have agreed with Wallace Stevens's claim that "death is the mother of beauty" and that a realm of heavenly perfection devoid of change would be boring.

> Is there no change of death in paradise?
> Does ripe fruit never fall? Or do the boughs

Hang always heavy in that perfect sky,
Unchanging, yet so like our perishing earth,
With rivers like our own that seek for seas
They never find.[4]

"A static value, however serious and important," Whitehead says, "becomes unendurable by its appalling monotony of endurance" (*SMW*, 202).[5] If modeled on the goal of attaining and sustaining some static value, civilization will fall into decline. Life requires "expansion and novelty" (*AI*, 81). Change, says Whitehead, is the fertilizer of the soul. "The soul cries aloud for a release into change. It suffers the agonies of claustrophobia" (*SMW*, 202).

Implied in Whitehead's view is the idea that finitude, transience, and process are necessary ingredients for the creation of a meaningful experience. As we will discuss later, Whitehead does say that a "merely finite" experience is trivial, *but* we must also realize that the "merely infinite" is a vacuous concept. "Those theologians do religion a bad service who emphasize infinitude at the expense of the finite transitions within history" (*MT*, 79). Existence is meaningless when the notions of process, creation, and change are not included as concepts descriptive of our metaphysical situation. "A frozen, motionless universe can at most be the topic of pure knowledge, with the bare comment—That is so" (*MT*, 80).

One of the reasons Nietzsche opposes what he calls "improvement-morality" is its stance toward the "negative qualities"—namely, suffering. Improvement-morality interprets these qualities as utterly undesirable and, more important, unnecessary. Their presence suggests a refutation of meaningfulness. Therefore, improvement-morality presents a scheme that purports to be capable of delivering one out of these qualities and to a reality where they do not exist. Improvement morality is nihilistic because, for Nietzsche, the character of reality is that such an escape is possible only at the expense of an attempt to remove oneself from existence. Nietzsche states improvement-morality is based on the misunderstanding that the positive quality can be isolated and enjoyed without any semblance of its opposite. When attempted, it results only in a tame and prosaic "comfort" that has no depth or profundity.

Whitehead largely agrees with Nietzsche on this point. One cannot remove or escape the condition for the possibility of suffering and evil without removing the condition for the possibility of happiness and beauty. This is due to the fact that these conditions are the same. "The categories governing the determination of things are the reasons why there should be evil; and are also the reasons why, in the advance of the world, particular evil facts are finally transcended" (*PR*, 223). Both evil and beauty are composed out of discord. The primary difference between them resides in the manner in which an actual entity deals with the discord. Whitehead defines beauty as "patterned contrast." It is the successful and harmonious integration of a number of diverse factors. The greater the diversity or discord successfully harmonized, the greater the beauty.

For Whitehead, there are two types of evil. The first is defined as a "discordant feeling" (*AI*, 256). This feeling has two or more discordant elements that clash to the point of "mutual destructiveness" (*AI*, 256). In this case, discord remains discordant. There is no harmony or successful integration between clashing feelings. "This is the feeling of evil in the most general sense, namely physical pain or mental evil, such as sorrow, horror, dislike" (*AI*, 256).

Regarding the presence of discord as evil, it seems that Whitehead would suggest that we avoid evil by simply avoiding the possibility of discord, that we seek to minimize our contact with those elements that might cause a disruption.[6] But the problem with this approach is that the avoidance of discord results in the type of decadence described earlier. The attempt to avoid turmoil is the reaction against the adventure toward higher forms of experience. This decadence refers to Whitehead's other type of evil. In this case, evil is the "loss of the higher experience in favour of the lower experience" (*RM*, 95). What Whitehead means is that if we avoid the threat of discord, we also give up the opportunity for higher forms of experience. This type of reaction toward discord results in an "unnecessary triviality."[7] Discord can be avoided only if we inhibit the opportunity for adventures towards novel forms of beauty.

For Whitehead, beauty requires complexity and intensity. Without these characteristics, one can accomplish only trivial harmony. An experience is beautiful when it is able to harmonize a variety of diverse elements in such a way that their differences result in neither a vulgar discord nor a homogenized and trivial uniformity.

> [The good of the soul] resides in the realization of a strength of many feelings fortifying each other as they meet in the novel unity. Its evil lies in the clash of vivid feelings, denying to each other their proper expansion. Its triviality lies in the anesthesia by which evil is avoided. (*AI*, 275)

Although the absence of discord would mean that one would not suffer from physical pain, one runs the risk of suffering excruciating boredom. Without discord, there would be only the repetition of past achievements; there would be no novelty. We can escape the potential for suffering only if we risk the evil of unnecessary triviality. Whitehead would agree that improvement-morality is based on a misunderstanding, and any attempt to carry it out would imply that there is no value in a world of Becoming. Beauty and evil are intermingled (*AI*, 259). Finitude and discord are necessary ingredients in any meaningful experience.

But where Whitehead differs from Nietzsche in an important way is that he does *not* see the development of democracy as a factor that produces "tame" and tensionless human beings who have no reverence for human life. On the contrary, for Whitehead, democracy is the outcome of an increased sense of the "dignity of man" (*AI*, 83). The ability to proffer respect for other human beings on the basis of their sheer humanity and to create a political structure that moves its constituents by persuasion is, for Whitehead, a sign of progress.

But, we should not understand Whitehead's views of democracy as the advocacy of a flattening of values. There is a moment in Price's *Dialogues* where Whitehead is reported as saying that democracy is in some sense responsible for a degree of "leveling" all things to a common denominator. "But while this concern for common people distinguishes our period and is one of its admirable traits. . . . [T]here is the question of whether more widely diffused opportunity will not depress talent and genius to less exalted levels" (*DLG*, 271). He then goes on to suggest that English and American interpretations of democracy are "unimaginative" (*DLG*, 272). These statements suggest that Whitehead's understanding of democracy in its ideal form is by no means the culturally relativistic sort where everything (thus nothing) is worthy of equal respect.

Christian Theology and the Static Absolute

Turning our attention back to theology, it is not necessarily the whole story to suggest that Christian theology constructs its doctrine of God on the axiom that God is absolutely immutable. The doctrines of the Trinity and the Incarnation have their basis in the idea of an active immanence of God in the world, thus offering a corrective to Plato's otherworldliness. For example, the orthodox rejection of Arius's view of God and Christ is evidence of the inadequacy of a wholesale Platonism for Christian theology. So concerned to protect the oneness of God and God's transcendence, Arius rejected the idea of a single essence shared by God and Christ alike. Whitehead writes, "There can be no doubt that the Arian solution, involving a derivative Image, is orthodox Platonism, though it be heterodox Christianity" (*AI*, 168). Plato, as we saw, was forced to admit a gap between the transient realm of particulars and the eternal realm of Forms. "The world, for Plato, includes only the image of God, and imitations of his ideas, and never God and his ideas" (*AI*, 168). Whitehead states that Christianity is to be credited because it tinkers with the idea of discerning a new relationship between God and the world, one that demands a doctrine of real immanence. "In place of Plato's solution of secondary images and imitations, they demanded a direct doctrine of immanence" (*AI*, 169).

Unfortunately, the early theologians botched this effort and "never made this advance into general metaphysics" (*AI*, 169). In the end, they only reinforced Plato's idea of the static absolute that is related only superficially to the world. "In the final metaphysical sublimation, [God] became the one absolute, omnipotent, omniscient source of all being, for his own existence requiring no relations to anything beyond himself" (*AI*, 169). This occurred because, Whitehead writes, "the nature of God was exempted from all the metaphysical categories which applied to the individual things in this temporal world" (*AI*, 169). In other words, there was no revision of the conceptual logic between permanence and flux used by Plato. Christian theologians still construed them as antithetical to one another. "They made no effort to conceive the World in terms of the metaphysical categories by means of which they interpreted God, and they made no effort to conceive God in terms of the metaphysical categories which they applied to the World" (*AI*, 169). Thus, God absolutely transcends the world and is absolutely permanent, exhibiting no change or relativity. As in Plato, at the heart of the classical doctrine of God is a denigration of the world of transience and change. "For them, God was eminently real, and the World was derivatively real. God was necessary to the World, but the World was not necessary to God. There was a gulf between them" (*AI*, 169).[8]

Ethical Problems with the Classical Doctrine of God

This formative period in Christian theology ends in failure.

> The failure consisted in the fact that the barbaric elements and the de-
> fects in intellectual comprehension had not been discarded, but re-
> mained as essential elements in the various formulations of Christian
> theology, orthodox and heretical alike. (*AI*, 166)

The defects in intellectual comprehension are those that stem from
the understanding of God as wholly eternal and permanent. By "barbaric elements," Whitehead is referring to the manner in which God's
power was understood. Because God is given all of the "positive"
concepts, God's power must be absolute, not relative; God must be
omnipotent. God's power came to be construed in the terms of
"Egyptian, Persian, and Roman imperial rulers" (*PR*, 342). As Whitehead writes, "The church gave unto God the attributes which be-
longed exclusively to Caesar" (*PR*, 342). If God is the sole power in
the universe, the entire world depends on God for its existence,
whereas God's existence depends on nothing. "He stood in the same
relation to the whole World as early Egyptian or Mesopotamian kings
stood to their subject populations" (*AI*, 169).

From this conception of God follow a number of ethical difficulties
that Whitehead objects to. His main objection is that this doctrine of
God is extremely problematic for the problem of evil.

> If this conception be adhered to, there can be no alternative except to
> discern in Him the origin of all evil as well as of all good. He is then the
> supreme author of the play, and to Him must therefore be ascribed its
> shortcomings as well as its success. (*SMW*, 179)

If God is omnipotent in the sense of being the *sole* power in the universe, one has difficulty in coherently affirming God's goodness and
God's exemption from responsibility for the existence of evil in the
world. As the sole power of the universe, God is responsible for all
occurrences in the world, thus making God accountable for evil. This
area of Whitehead's criticism of God has been well documented and
developed by Whitehead's followers.[9] In the remainder of this chapter, I would like to consider how Whitehead holds that the traditional
doctrine of God is largely incapable of eliciting a response that exhibits an affirmation of humanity and life in the world. This discussion

will show that Whitehead's concerns with the traditional doctrine of God parallel those of Nietzsche's concerns.

The Response of Fear

As I stated, fundamental to the traditional doctrine of God is the idea of omnipotence, which states that God is the sole locus of power. The world is the free and arbitrary creation of God, and nothing in the world can have any constitutive influence on God. God influences without being influenced. God's existence does not depend on anything. This understanding of God's power has, Whitehead writes, "infused tragedy into the histories of Christianity and Mahometanism" (*PR*, 342). The stress on God's coercive power led to the image of God as an "imperial ruler" (*PR*, 342) and an "absolute tyrant" (*AI*, 169).

A likely response of human beings who accept this God is one of fear. "The Christian world was composed of terrified populations" (*RM*, 75). Terrifying them was the fear of the vengeance of the flaming fire on those "that know not God" and will be punished with everlasting destruction (*RM*, 75).[10] As a despot, God's will must be obeyed. The value and significance of individual human beings are slight under the authority of this God. One's life is that of a slave, living only for the whims of the master. Under the constant threat of fear one is not likely to affirm one's life in this world as intrinsically valuable. This understanding of God conflicts, Whitehead says, with the understanding of "God as love" (*RM*, 75). He blames this view on the influence of Paul.

In this respect, Whitehead would agree with Nietzsche's criticism of the "moral world order." Connected to the idea of God as a tyrant is the notion of God as a "ruthless moralist" (*PR*, 343). Of course, Whitehead is not opposed to the idea that religious beliefs carry with them certain codes of conduct. The problem is that the moral imperatives of a tyrannical God have very little to do with any ideal concerning the goodness of human life in the world. In the case of a tyrannical God, goodness is defined on strictly moral terms. That which is good is that which adheres to the ordained code of conduct. This is not a morality designed to increase the enjoyment of individual actual entities in the world. It is a morality that stands outside and against humanity, thus requiring the repression of an individual's own needs and desires.[11] One follows the rules of a tyrant only out of fear of punishment. One lives for God yet cannot participate in God.

It might be suggested that the fear of God is not without its rewards, for such fear is partially motivated by the promise that obedience will be rewarded with the gift of eternal bliss. Nietzsche entertained this question and answered with some thoughts about the
content of this sort of hope. He concluded that we would be justified
in thinking that above the gateway to Christian paradise should be
the inscription "I too was created by eternal *hate*" (*GM*, I:15). Quoting Aquinas and Tertullian, Nietzsche states that the bliss of paradise
is constituted by the enjoyment of seeing the damned punished (*GM*,
I:15).[12] This attitude is further evidence that at the heart of the psychology of the Christian is a deep feeling of *ressentiment*. Whitehead
is equally outraged by these sentiments. "Must 'religion' always remain as a synonym for 'hatred?'" (*AI*, 172). Far more preferable to the
apocalyptic vision of the last book of the Bible, *Revelations*, with "its
barbaric elements," is, Whitehead writes, the "Funeral Speech" of
Pericles, with its passionate defense of Athenian democratic principles. "Yet it is shocking to think that [*Revelations*] has been retained
for the formation of religious sentiment, while the speech of Pericles,
descriptive of the Athenian ideal of civilization, has remained neg-
lected in this connection" (*AI*, 170).

Nietzsche complained that one of the consequences of monotheis-
tic religion, as opposed to those that were polytheistic, is that it
brought about the "doctrine of one normal human type" (*GS*, 143).
The great danger of this doctrine is that it does not permit a "plurality
of norms," which Nietzsche thinks is required for human flourishing.
For Nietzsche, human flourishing requires that one be able to posit
one's own ideals. "Let us finally consider how naïve it is altogether to
say: 'Man *ought* to be such and such!' Reality shows us an enchanting
wealth of types, the abundance of a lavish play and change of forms"
(*TI*, "Morality as Anti-Nature," 6).

Whitehead lodges a similar complaint. This concept of God has led
to the unfortunate tendency of absolutizing morality so that it becomes dogmatic and inflexible. "Moral codes have suffered from the
exaggerated claims made for them. . . . Each such code has been put
out by a God on a mountain top, or by a saint in a cave, or by a divine Despot on a throne" (*AI*, 290). The absolutizing of morality
makes it seem as if there is only one proper way of behaving. Part of
Whitehead's objection to a dogmatic morality is that it can give way
to the sort of decadence we saw with Plato's desire for static permanence. Whitehead writes, "the champions of morality are on the

whole the fierce opponents of new ideals" (*AI*, 269). Dogmatic morality can stop growth and the impulse toward higher forms of experience. For Whitehead, reality is multifarious and in constant process.
Therefore, "there is not just one ideal 'order' which all actual entities
should attain and fail to attain. In each case, there is an ideal peculiar
to each particular actual entity" (*PR*, 84). And with a bit more precision, he writes:

> Each society has its own type of perfection. . . . Thus the notion that
> there are certain regulative notions, sufficiently precise to prescribe de-
> tails of conduct, for all reasonable beings on Earth, in every planet, and
> in every star-system, is at once to be put aside. (*AI*, 291)

The rise of absolutism is problematic because it leads to a denial of
adventure.[13] An inflexible, dogmatic morality can arrest development.
Openness and tolerance are necessary ingredients in the advance of
the universe. "The duty of tolerance is our finite homage to the abundance of inexhaustible novelty which is awaiting the future, and to
the complexity of accomplished fact which exceeds our stretch of in-
sight" (*AI*, 52). So although Whitehead's doctrine of God is monothe-
istic, this doctrine is squared, as we will see in chapter 8, with the
need for "homage to the abundance of inexhaustible novelty."

The Response of Resignation

Another possible response to the traditional doctrine of God is that
of resignation. The response of resignation or abandonment does not
center so much on the idea of God as a tyrant but on the absolute gulf
between eminent reality and this world of change, strife, and turmoil.
Due to the fact that God and heaven were construed as absolutely different in kind from this world, Whitehead believed that many Christians were led to disregard this world and to accept the fact that the
realization of one's ideal aim can come only when one escapes this
world. There has always been the "temptation to abandon the immediate experience of this world as a lost cause" (*AI*, 32). In other words,
this doctrine of God leads to otherworldliness.

> In the hands of theologians both in the Middle Age and in the first pe-
> riod of its supersession, the Platonic-Christian tradition leant heavily to-
> wards its mystical religious side. It abandoned this world to the Evil
> Prince therof [*sic*], and concentrated thought upon another world and a
> better life. (*AI*, 32)

This abandonment is due in part to the presupposition that anything involved in turmoil is evil. Thus, in a world that is in a state of constant change, no meaning can be achieved. When eminent reality is construed to be absolutely different in kind from this world of Becoming, the response it elicits is that one is to "be tranquil" with the faith that "the shadows pass" (*AI*, 33). In this scenario, the economy of Christian life can only be one of escape from this world; one yearns for rest and quiet. Part of the problem here is that the contrasting notions of "strife" and "harmony" are understood as antithetical concepts, thus leading one to believe that only one of them can be indicative of ultimate reality. Classical theology took "harmony," understood here as a static tranquility, to be the sign of ultimate reality. Because the finite world is thought to be characterized solely by strife, renunciation of the world is necessary because no such tranquility can be found in the world.

It is interesting to note that Whitehead traces a development in the concept of God from Judaism to Christianity similar to Nietzsche's. For Nietzsche, the evolution of the concept of God is a process of "denaturalization," by which he means that it goes from a concept that serves life to one that is so transcendent of the world that it becomes hostile to life. Expressing a similar view, Whitehead writes, "For the early Hebrews, their God was a personage whose aims were expressible in terms of the immediate political and social circumstances. Their religious notions had singularly slight reference to another World" (*AI*, 81). In early Christianity, there begins a "disregard of temporal fact" and the "abstraction of ideals" (*AI*, 81). In other words, the ideals aimed at are otherworldly.

> The translation of Eastern modes of thought—Semitic, Greek, and Egyptian—to Western Europe had the unfortunate effect of making the ideal side of civilization appear more abstract than it was in the lands and the epochs of its origin. (*AI*, 81)

The Search for Comfort

A third response possible under the umbrella of this doctrine of God is the search for comfort. This more modern reaction appeared at a time when the fear of God as a tyrant was losing its ability to draw people to religion. Science was making many of religion's claims dubious. Under pressure from secular critics, theologians had come to abandon many of the tenets of classical theology, most notably those associated with theology's supernaturalism. But this more liberal theology does not represent much of an improvement, especially in regard to the response it is capable of eliciting from its followers.

The motives of religion have become aligned with the motive of technological science, which is "the desire for a comfortable organization of modern society" (*SMW*, 191). The function of religion is merely to serve as "a sanction to right conduct" (*SMW*, 191). The dogmatic claims of religion, built on the foundation of a supernaturalistic cosmology, have been weakened to the point where the "procedure ends by basing religion on those few ideas which in the circumstances of the time are most effective in producing pleasing emotions and agreeable conduct" (*RM*, 77).

Although Whitehead gives almost no historical details of this development, we can suggest that he has in mind those liberal theologies of the eighteenth and nineteenth centuries that had attempted to reformulate the content of Christian doctrine along the lines of those dominating scientific beliefs based in a materialistic (and now atheistic) naturalism. By both denying supernaturalism and accepting this form of naturalism, they were forced to all but empty many of Christianity claims. Commenting on these events, David Griffin writes:

> Modern liberal theology developed its thinness when the acceptance of sensationism and the mechanistic view of nature was combined with the rejection of supernaturalism and dualism in favor of a more or less completely materialistic worldview with no room for divine influence, life after death, and most of the other beliefs that have been associated with robust religion.[14]

Although this response seems to be more banal than the others, it results in some of the same problems. Here, we still have the understanding of God and religion that engender a life of decadence. When religion is thought of as only providing a formula for a comfortable life with pleasing social relations, religion cannot function in the way Whitehead thinks it ought to. For Whitehead, religion ought to lead to an "adventure of the spirit," and not a "rule of safety" (*SMW*, 192). Like the decadence involved in Plato's desire for a static absolute, the religion in search of comfort seeks only to maintain order. Adventure, we remember, requires discord and an occasional obliviousness towards morality. Furthermore, although God is not construed as a tyrant, individuals are still presumed to be subordinated to a preordained conception of orderliness. It is thought that human life is a project of adjusting ourselves to an external moral code. "The insistence upon rules of conduct marks the ebb of religious fervour" (*SMW*, 191).

It can also be suggested that the life of the search for comfort is similar to the life of Nietzsche's "last man." The situations are similar. The last man takes the nature of reality to be such that no great accomplishments can be achieved and seeks only to organize life so that at least discomfort can be avoided. Whitehead's religion in search of comfort accepts the same banal picture of reality, believing only that religion can provide an (empty and insipid) morality that minimizes tensions.

CONCLUSION

In all three of these responses, human life becomes a project of maintaining and conserving order. Life in the world, if it is to be engaged at all, is to be approached defensively or, in Nietzsche's terms, "ascetically." Christian life, when revolving around the traditional doctrine of God, is checkered with a destructive decadence similar to the sort we saw going on with Plato. Because the primary characteristic of reality is process, life demands "expansion and novelty" (*AI*, 81). The policy of "sociological defence is doomed to failure" (*AI*, 80). Insofar as God is defined in terms of a static absolute, the desire for adventure must be repressed. "The death of religion comes with the repression of the high hope of adventure" (*SMW*, 192).

NOTES

1. Hartshorne, *Omnipotence and Other Theological Mistakes* (Albany: State University of New York Press, 1984), 44.

2. See Griffin, *Religion and Scientific Naturalism: Overcoming the Conflicts* (Albany: State University of New York Press, 2000), 96.

3. Whitehead suggests that the idea that mathematical entities are devoid of process is mistaken. Plato misunderstands mathematics when he identifies it with a realm of changeless eternity. Whitehead writes "that mathematics is concerned with certain forms of process issuing into forms which are components for further process" (*MT*, 92). It should be clear that White-

head's critique of Greek mathematics is not directed at either mathematics' general usefulness or even its ability to illuminate various aspects of the nature of reality. Rather, it is directed at a specific view of mathematics. What Whitehead is leery of is what Ralph Norman calls *mathematicism*. Mathematicism involves the presupposition that knowledge is only that which is deductively certain. Whitehead's interest in mathematics is, as Norman writes, in its "*aesthetic* philosophical use—i.e., its use as the search for infinitely rich and diverse patterns of order, in its confidence that the conception and enjoyment of such coherence is an open-ended enterprise, that in fact the mind deployed has as its destiny whatever expansion of its initial systems may be required in the large encounter of looking and finding" (Ralph V. Norman Jr., "Whitehead and 'Mathematicism,'" in *Alfred North Whitehead: Essays on His Philosophy*, ed. George L. Kline [Englewood Cliffs, N.J.: Prentice Hall, 1963], 34).

4. Wallace Stevens, "Sunday Morning," in *The Collected Poems* (New York: Vintage, 1982), 69.

5. When asked what he would do in heaven, Whitehead reportedly replied that he would rather go to "Limbo" (*DLG*, 134). After Whitehead's comment, Mrs. Whitehead was said to have wondered how anyone could endure the "mortal tedium of heaven" (*DLG*, 134).

6. See David Griffin, *God, Power, and Evil: A Process Theodicy* (Philadelphia: Westminster, 1976), 282–85.

7. Griffin, *God, Power, and Evil*, 285.

8. Whitehead gives little historical evidence for this account. Fortunately, Whitehead's views can be corroborated by recent work in the area of historical theology. Jaroslav Pelikan extensively catalogues the great difficulties, especially in the areas of Christology and the Trinity, encountered by early Christian theologians because of their felt need to uphold the axiom of God as absolutely immutable. See *The Christian Tradition: A History of the Development of Doctrine*, vol. 1, *The Emergence of the Catholic Tradition*, 229–32. Also, Charles Hartshorne has shown the religious and philosophical untenablity of this classical doctrine of God. See "Introduction: The Standpoint of Panentheism" in *Philosophers Speak of God*, 1–15.

9. For example, see Griffin, *God, Power, and Evil*, and Marjorie Suchocki, *The End of Evil: Process Eschatology in Historical Context* (Albany: State University of New York Press, 1988).

10. Whitehead is quoting II Thess. 1:8–9.

11. John Cobb makes this point in *God and the World* (Philadelphia: Westminster, 1969), 28.

12. Nietzsche quotes passages from Aquinas, *Summa Theologiae*, III, *Supplementum*, Q. 94, Art. 1, and Tertullian, *De Spectaculis*.

13. John Cobb articulates a similar sentiment: "I experienced the undermining of the seriousness of moral obligation as the threat of existential nihilism,

but I experienced the life of moral seriousness as restrictive and burdensome. Hence it was just as important to relativize ethics as to affirm its seriousness." See "Response to Reynolds," in *John Cobb's Theology in Process*, ed. David Ray Griffin and Thomas J. J. Altizer (Philadelphia: Westminster, 1977), 181–82.

14. Griffin, *Religion and Scientific Naturalism: Overcoming the Conflicts*, 230.

7

The Life and Sense of the World

In the remaining chapters of this study, I want to discuss Whitehead's positive views of religion, especially his understanding of religious experience and the relationship between God and the meaning of human life. Along the way I hope to show that Whitehead's understanding of these matters is not subject to Nietzsche's criticism of the Christian doctrine of God as "life-denying." In fact, Whitehead's view of the religious life bears several important similarities to Nietzsche's views of the possibilities for human life after the death of God.

Before explicitly discussing Whitehead's doctrine of God, it is necessary to look at some of the more general and wider aspects of his philosophy. My concern in this chapter is twofold. First, I discuss Whitehead's criticism of what he understands to be the dominant worldview and its supporting epistemology. Second, I show what Whitehead offers as an alternative. This discussion is crucial for the more detailed comments regarding Whitehead's view of religion and God.

WHITEHEAD'S CRITICISM OF SCIENTIFIC MATERIALISM

Whitehead's writings (at least those from 1925 on)[1] are imbued with concerns about the current state of modern society and the influence of what he takes to be the dominant worldview on the lives and practices of human beings. "At the present time," he writes, "as

at other epochs, society is decaying, and there is need for preser-
vative action" (*SMW*, 204–5). Society, he thinks, is in a current state
of decline because it is unable to offer individuals—through its social institutions and its dominant intellectual discourses—a sense
that life in the world is intrinsically valuable and that their actions
are meaningful. The modern worldview teaches human beings that
the world itself is bleak, purposeless, and barren. It encourages human beings to think only of themselves and to pursue their lives in
isolation both from others and the surrounding environment. Furthermore, the epistemology of the modern worldview assumes a
certain estrangement or gap between human experience and reality. When Whitehead writes that the purpose of his lecture "Civilized Universe" in *Modes of Thought* is to provide evidence "for that
concept of the universe which is the justification for the ideals char-
acterizing civilized phases of human society," he is expressing a
concern that the currently dominant view of reality provides no
such justification (*MT*, 105). In short, for Whitehead the modern
worldview bars human beings from the very things or conditions
that make a meaningful and valuable life possible.

In these later writings, the dominant problems that Whitehead ad-
dresses are those that stem from philosophical interpretations of nature. In *Modes of Thought*, he writes that "*the status of life* in nature
. . . is the modern problem of philosophy and science" (*MT*, 148). We
need to think about the status of life in nature, he says, because
trends of thought that emerged in the seventeenth century, then became more dominant in the eighteenth and nineteenth centuries, finally being institutionalized in the domain of public discourse in the
early twentieth century, have resulted in a separation of "nature" and
"life."[2] By "nature," here understood narrowly to be the world as interpreted through categories provided by sensory perception, Whitehead is referring to what is commonly called the "physical world"
(*MT*, 128). "Life," by contrast, refers to that which exhibits a sense of
"self-enjoyment," "freedom," "creativity," "purpose," and "subjectivity." Life, he writes, "is the enjoyment of emotions derived from the
past and aimed at the future" (*MT*, 167).[3]

In the early seventeenth century, a general consensus arose that nature, in the sense of the physical world, was "lifeless." This consensus,
called "scientific materialism" or "mechanistic materialism," forms the
basis of modern science. In *Science and the Modern World*, Whitehead gives a brief summary of its general assumptions:

There persists, however, throughout the whole period the fixed scientific cosmology which presupposes the ultimate fact of an irreducible brute matter, or material, spread throughout space in a flux of configurations. In itself such a material is senseless, valueless, purposeless. It just does what it does, following a fixed routine imposed by external relations which do not spring from the nature of its being. (*SMW*, 17)

In addition, these bits of matter are isolated individuals, related to other bits of matter only externally. Matter, or nature, exhibits no capacity for creativity, spontaneity, self-movement, or novelty. Nature is a "self-sufficient meaningless complex of facts" (*MT*, 132). This view of nature came to the fore through the work of Galileo, Mersenne, Descartes, Boyle, and Newton.

Although scientific materialism has long been associated with a nontheistic interpretation of the natural world, this has not always been the case. In fact, most of those thinkers responsible for bringing this view of nature to the forefront (especially Mersenne, Descartes, Boyle, and Newton) did so precisely because it seemed the best possible worldview for protecting and sustaining the very religious beliefs that gave their lives meaning. The twin notions that the laws of nature are externally imposed and that bits of matter are only externally related to one another suggest, Whitehead writes, "a certain type of Deism, and conversely it is the outcome of such a Deistic belief if already entertained" (*AI*, 113). Whitehead is suggesting that originally the assumption that bits of matter are lifeless, exhibiting no sense of freedom, supported the traditional theological idea that God is omnipotent, which we discussed in the previous chapter.[4] By presuming that nature was lifeless, one could argue that the natural world is wholly subservient to God's power. Newton, he writes, "definitely stated that the correlated modes of behaviour of the bodies forming the solar system required God for the imposition of the principles on which all depended" (*AI*, 113). Because the things of nature are now in motion, there must be some source for these activities, hence God. This is Newton's version of the cosmological argument for the existence of God.[5] The idea that there are fixed laws governing the activities of material bodies, with no room for irregularity, spontaneity, or freedom, is "without interest apart from the correlative doctrine of a transcendent imposing Deity" (*AI*, 113).

In another example given by Whitehead, the view of lifeless, valueless nature is shown to be important for the Protestant Reformation. The presumption that nature is valueless, he writes, "is illustrated in the recoil of Protestantism from aesthetic effects dependent upon a material medium" (*SMW*, 195). Many Protestant doctrines were sustained by maintaining that the material world has no value except insofar as it is suggestive of an omnipotent God. In the next sentence, he comments on what the idea of an animated, intrinsically valuable environment was thought to be indicative of: "It was taken to lead to an ascription of value to what is in itself valueless" (*SMW*, 195). Put another way, the ascription of value to nature was seen as a threat to God's eminent status. In both of these examples, the valuelessness and lifelessness of nature are posited in the name of granting greater value and power to God. The value of this world is lessened to heighten the value of an otherworldly divine entity.

Other core doctrines were at stake as well. If nature had life, not only would God's omnipotence be threatened but so, too, would the belief that the soul was immortal. While nature and bodies were thought to be lifeless, the qualities of life were attributed solely to immaterial minds or souls. In the thinking of Boyle and Descartes, the idea that matter contained self-motion and experience threatened the qualitative difference between souls and bodies. Mortalists could argue that because the body is composed of self-moving things yet is subject to decay, the soul's capacity for subjectivity and freedom is no guarantee of its immortality.[6]

THE EPISTEMOLOGY OF SCIENTIFIC MATERIALISM

Supporting the cosmology of scientific materialism is a particular epistemology, which Whitehead calls the "sensationalist doctrine of perception." According to this epistemology, experience of the world beyond one's own mind is thought to be completely rooted in sense perception. The world that can be construed on the basis of sense perception is barren, devoid of any enjoyment, aim, and purpose. Sense perception is limited to what Whitehead calls "perception in the mode of presentational immediacy," and it is only aware of the immediate present. Presentational immediacy, Whitehead writes, "gives no information as to the past or future. It merely presents an illustrated portion of the presented duration" (*PR*, 168). For example, in the perception of a grey stone, "what is directly perceived, certainly and without shadow of doubt, is a grey region of the presented locus" (*PR*, 172). There is no indication that the present emerges out of the past and is headed toward the future. There is, it seems, nothing going on in nature.

It is partly because of its commitment to the sensationalist doctrine of perception that scientific materialism accepts the notion that bits of matter are static and vacuous. "Science can find no individual enjoyment in nature: Science can find no aim in nature: Science can find no creativity in nature" (*MT*, 154). Sensationism does not, neither of itself nor especially when used in conjunction with a supernaturalistic view of God that is omnipotent, give us any evidence of any qualities that are suggestive of purposive behavior on the part of the constituents of nature. Furthermore, it disallows one from connecting certain value experiences—namely, aesthetic and ethical—to an experience of something going on in the world.

The Nonsense of Aesthetics

Allegiance to the sensationalist doctrine of perception requires that we conclude that aesthetic values are cognitively meaningless. According to scientific materialism, matter is valueless (*SMW*, 17). The bits of matter, constituting what is thought to be the ultimate units of reality, do not have most of the qualities they are perceived to have, such as color, scent, or sound. For Descartes, the only quality attributed to matter was extension. Newton added mass and others added motion. "Nature is left with bits of matter, qualified by mass, spatial relations, and the change of such relations" (*MT*, 132). These qualities are said to be "primary" in the sense of being really out there in reality. All other qualities are thought either to be "secondary" or "tertiary," not essentially out there in reality.

Scientific materialism accounts for these secondary and tertiary qualities by suggesting that they are merely subjective reactions to sensory stimulation. All that is going on in nature is the simple movement of matter (*SMW*, 53). About Galileo, Whitehead writes, "Galileo considered this question, and at once pointed out that apart from eyes, ears, or noses, there would be no colours, sounds, or smells" (*SMW*, 53). For Locke, "these sensations are projected by the mind so as to clothe appropriate bodies in external nature" (*SMW*, 54). The world is really bare, made to seem colorful and the like only by the mind. In scientific materialism, "nature is a dull affair, soundless, scentless, colourless; merely the hurrying of material, endlessly, meaninglessly" (*SMW*, 54). As David Griffin notes, a mechanistic, materialistic view of nature is "disenchanted."[7] Nature is not an inherently aesthetic place. Any intuition we have about the beauty of nature cannot be said to be true or false. Although scientific materialism does not deny that such feelings occur, its inability to connect them to objects in the world makes it difficult to see how they might provide one with the sense that life *in the world* is meaningful. The modern worldview anesthetizes both the world and humanity. In a disenchanted world of dead nature, the "poets are entirely mistaken" (*SMW*, 54). In such a world, the credit for the existence of beauty belongs, not to nature, but to "the excellency of the human mind" (*SMW*, 54).

When aesthetic sensibilities are divorced from reality, Whitehead notes, art is treated as a "frivolity." The presupposition that "matter in motion is the one concrete reality in nature" means that "aesthetic values form an adventitious, irrelevant addition" (*SMW*, 204). If nature is valueless, there is no reason either to revere natural or artistic beauty or to orient our practices around such values (*SMW*, 196). Aesthetic activities have no serious place in society, except insofar as they might contribute to survival value.[8]

An epistemology that is incapable of connecting "secondary" qualities to nature has given society the nihilistic "habit of ignoring the intrinsic worth of the environment" (*SMW*, 196). Because aesthetic values are thought to be unreal, their cultivation is thought to do nothing to increase the quality of life. In the modern worldview, Whitehead says, being in touch with reality means being in contact with "*things* as opposed to *values*" (*SMW*, 202). For Whitehead, if human beings are denied the cultivation of aesthetic intuitions, the quality of human life suffers greatly. Art, he says, "transforms the soul into the permanent realisation of values extending beyond its former self" (*SMW*, 202). It introduces us to interesting lures that can inspire new ways of being in the world. Art fertilizes the soul, providing it with the means for attaining experiences of greater depth and intensity. The modern worldview, however, makes aesthetic values unimportant.

The Nonsense of Ethics

Along with the relegation of aesthetic intuitions to the realm of nonsense go also any of our ethical feelings. First, this epistemology, as exemplified by David Hume, makes it entirely difficult to assert the existence of some sort of soul to human beings. Every moment of introspection reveals, Hume thought, only that "I" am aware of having various impressions. There is never a moment when "I" can catch myself lacking an impression. Nor is there ever a perception of the self or soul. Therefore, he concluded, the self, soul, or mind is nothing other than this loose bundle of impressions. The identity we ascribe to ourselves is fictitious. Hume writes, "I may venture to affirm of the rest of mankind that they are nothing but a bundle or collection of different perceptions, which succeed each other with an inconceivable rapidity and are in a perpetual flux and movement."[9] In the wake of this anthropology, says Whitehead, "the status of man in the universe required re-considering" (*AI*, 29). If human beings are nothing more than a bundle of isolated impressions, there is no longer any coherent way to talk about personal identity.[10]

The loss of any identifiable agent and any locus of a peculiarly high grade of intrinsic value makes ethics difficult. For example, the early Christians, Whitehead states, could argue against the institution of slavery because of their assumption that God created all human beings with a soul. But with Hume, Whitehead writes, "there seems to be no very obvious reason why one flux of impressions should not be related to another flux of impressions in the relative status of master to slave" (*AI*, 30). If human beings have no soul, what is being violated by enslavement? To be sure, Hume did not defend slavery, but with the loss of an identifiable agent, he could give no theoretical justification for abolishing it.

In addition to leaving us without any basis for the respect of human beings qua human beings, Hume's epistemology makes nonsense of ethical feelings in general. Because of his commitment to the sensationalist epistemology, Hume must deny the primacy of emotional experience, regarding emotional feelings as nothing more than psychological reactions to sense data (PR, 141). When this sensationalist epistemology is accepted, "the mass of our moral, emotional, and purposive experience is rendered trivial and accidental" (*MT*, 109). The fact that one feels an ethical connection—for example, a feeling of love or sympathy—to another human being or the world at large is explained only as a private reaction to a sense perception, not an intuition of the intrinsic value of others. "For Hume, hating, loving, thinking, feeling, are nothing but perceptions derivative from these fundamental [sense] impressions" (*PR*, 146).

Unable to connect emotional experience to something going on in reality, the sensationalist doctrine of perception leads to problems of moral relativism. In a statement about Descartes but equally applicable to Hume, Whitehead says that "the moral intuitions can be held to apply only to the strictly private world of psychological experience" (*SMW*, 196). For Hume, our moral decisions do not come about by means of a rational inquiry into the nature of the Good. Reason is unable to demonstrate the goodness of some situation or action because such qualities, he thinks, do not exist outside the mind. For Hume, our moral codes refer to private sentiments. Therefore, there can be no metaphysical principle of ethical ideals. Since no "ought" can in any sense be rooted in an "is," there can be no standard for adjudicating actions. "A solipsist experience," Whitehead writes, "cannot succeed or fail, for it would be all that exists" (*MT*, 103).

Although Hume attacked the foundation for ethics, he still attempted to give it a sort of objectivity. Certain values—namely, sympathy and benevolence—have been passed on from generation to generation, thereby giving them an air of universality. For Hume, it is the universality of these sentiments that serves as the moral standard. But, again, this sentiment of sympathy does not come through an experience of reality. Rather, the ideal is purely a matter of custom, and the passion for other human beings is assumed to be limited. "In general, it may be affirm'd that there is no such passion in human minds," Whitehead quotes Hume as saying, "as the love of mankind, merely as such, independent of personal qualities, or services, or of relations to ourself" (*AI*, 30). Ethical ideals are understood as arbitrary decisions that have no basis in reality.

WHITEHEAD'S EPISTEMOLOGY AND THE SENSE OF AESTHETIC AND ETHICAL INTUITIONS

Whitehead's own epistemology does not require that one relegate aesthetic and ethical intuitions to a realm of nonsense, a realm of mere subjective experience that is not connected to an experience of the external world. The main error of sensationalist epistemology is that it is too narrow. "My quarrel with modern epistemology," Whitehead says, "concerns its exclusive stress upon sense perception for the provision of data respecting nature" (*MT*, 133). For Whitehead, human experience is composed of much more than the experience of sense-datum. Immediately prior to sense experience, or "perception in the mode of presentational immediacy," is a more primitive layer of experience. This is evident in that the data of the senses come to the mind through the mediation of our bodily organs. For example, the mind does not *see* the eye, but it does experience it. It *feels* the eye as the source of sight.[11] Whatever it is that we see, we see *with* our eyes. Even Hume, Whitehead reminds us, could not refrain from using this sort of language (*PR*, 81). Whitehead takes this fact to be evidence that we have "direct knowledge of the antecedent functioning of the body in sense-perception" (*PR*, 81). This direct knowledge involves a second mode of perception, which he calls "perception in the mode of causal efficacy." It differs from perception in the mode of presentational immediacy by pointing to a reality external to the mind. Our sense perceptions do not float in from nowhere but come to us through bodily experience. Some actual entities external to the mind are efficacious on its state of being.

Although our own bodies are the strongest source of these feelings, Whitehead extends the field of that which is causally efficacious to the entire past world. "The body is the starting point for our knowledge of the circumambient world" (*PR*, 81). Through perception in the mode of causal efficacy, one has "a direct perception of those antecedent actual occasions which are causally efficacious . . . for the percipient" (*PR*, 169).[12]

It is through perception in the mode of causal efficacy, which Hume and others have to deny because they equate perception with sense perception, that human beings can affirm that, at least to some degree, sense perception is an experience of an actual world, external to human subjectivity.[13] In a passage describing causal efficacy, worth quoting at length, Whitehead writes:

> [Perception in the mode of causal efficacy] produces the sense of derivation from an immediate past, and of passage to an immediate future; a sense of emotional feeling, belonging to oneself in the past, passing into oneself in the present, and passing from oneself in the present towards oneself in the future; a sense of influx of influence from other vaguer presences in the past, localized and yet evading local definition, such influence modifying, enhancing, inhibiting, diverting, the stream of feeling which we are receiving, unifying, enjoying, and transmitting. This is our general sense of existence, as one item among others, in an efficacious actual world. (*PR*, 178)

In the opening pages of Thomas Wolfe's novel *Look Homeward Angel*, we find a nice description of this sentiment:

> Each of us is all the sums he has not counted: subtract us into nakedness and night again, and you shall see begin in Crete four thousand

years ago the love that ended yesterday in Texas. . . . Each moment is the fruit of forty thousand years. The minute-winning days, like flies, buzz home to death, and every moment is a window on all time.[14]

For Whitehead, we are not isolated individuals enjoying private sensations.

Thus, unlike the sensationalist doctrine of perception, Whitehead's epistemology can show that human experience flows out of a causally efficacious environment. Our experiences are experiences of something other than ourselves. In contrast, acceptance of the sensationalist doctrine of perception involves a sense of alienation and disconnection.[15] "Orthodox philosophy can only introduce us to solitary substances, each enjoying an illusory experience: 'O Bottom, thou art changed! what do I see on thee?'" (*PR*, 50)[16] In *Symbolism*, Whitehead writes that "the mere presentational side of the world overwhelms with the sense of its emptiness" (*S*, 48). As an example of the despair involved in experience that cannot deliver a world, Whitehead cites a saying of William Pitt, prime minister of England during the French Revolution. Upon his death he is reported as having said, "What shades we are, what shadows we pursue!" Whitehead comments:

> His mind had suddenly lost the sense of causal efficacy, and was illuminated by the remembrance of the intensity of emotion, which had enveloped his life, in its comparison with the barren emptiness of the world passing in sense-presentation. (*S*, 48–49)

Without perception in the mode of causal efficacy, we feel as if we are floating, experiencing this or that. In an account of experience that limits itself to sense experience, the general feeling of living in a world fraught and imbued with significance and purpose does not arise because the connection between human beings and the world has been severed.

In a chapter of *Science and the Modern World* entitled "The Romantic Reaction," Whitehead discusses the Romantic rejection of the worldview of scientific materialism, in particular its assumption that the world is valueless. "The nature-poetry of the romantic revival was a protest on behalf of the organic view of nature, and also a protest against the exclusion of value from the essence of the matter of fact" (*SMW*, 94). In the poetry of Wordsworth and Shelley, Whitehead finds articulations of intuitions concerning the inherent value of nature. "Both Shelley and Wordsworth emphatically bear witness that nature cannot be divorced from its aesthetic values" (*SMW*, 87). Wordsworth, who was "passionately absorbed in nature," felt that the current mechanistic worldview of dead nature could not grasp "the important facts of nature" (*SMW*, 83). The theme of Wordsworth's *Prelude*, Whitehead writes, "is nature *in solido*, that is to say, he dwells on the mysterious presence of surrounding things, which imposes itself on any separate element that we set up as an individual for its own sake" (*SMW*, 83). Shelley writes with similar sentiments. "For Shelley nature retains its beauty and its colour. Shelley's nature is in its essence a nature of organisms, functioning with the full content of our perceptual experience" (*SMW*, 85).

What Whitehead so greatly appreciates about Wordsworth and Shelley is that they connected their enjoyment of aesthetic qualities to something really going on in nature. The experience of beauty is not wholly the production of human subjectivity. We experience beauty because something going on in nature makes this experience possible. In Whitehead's epistemology, "*things* pave the way for *cognition*" (*SMW*, 89).

To be sure, Whitehead accepts the idea that color as we see it and other qualities as experienced through our senses are not *in* the perceived entities. He is not a naïve realist. But he rejects the idea that these qualities are arbitrarily added by the perceiving mind. Secondary qualities correspond in some sense to the internal constitutions of the entities we perceive. As Griffin writes, they are "produced by the mind out of values, or emotions,"[17] not out of purely quantitative, vacuous things. In particular, they are, if they are accurate, produced by feeling what the perceived entity is feeling. As I discuss in the next section, for Whitehead, *all* actual entities have an inner reality. This inner reality is the achievement of some value. In a prehension of some actual entity in the past world we feel those values. "Occasion B prehends occasion A as an antecedent subject experiencing a sensum with emotional intensity" (*PR*, 315).

The greatness of the English Romantics lies in the fact that they understood their poetic experiences as indicative of the intrinsic value of nature. Whitehead suggests that the reason Wordsworth can feel "the brooding, immediate presence of things" is because our bodily experience is a unification of the entire past universe (*SMW*, 92). Because of the link between aesthetic enjoyment and intrinsic value, these poets were granted a sense of the meaningfulness of living in a world that is not merely a subjective construction. Life in the world for these poets is meaningful because what they see, smell, taste, and feel are experiences of things really going on in the world beyond the human mind's perceptions and conceptions. Wordsworth, says Whitehead, can laugh "with the daffodils" and "finds in the primrose thought 'too deep for tears'" (*SMW*, 83). This emotional sensitivity is unavailable to those with faculties enculturated in the worldview of scientific materialism. It is possible only when one presupposes that the world itself is fraught with value and that we can experience this value.

In regard to the cognitive status of our ethical feelings—for example, our feeling of sympathy—Whitehead's epistemology allows us to understand these feelings as having some truth. My feeling of sympathy is true in that through perception in the mode of causal efficacy I am aware that I am internally related to the past world. Sympathy, for Whitehead, is a metaphysical principle. I explain this in more detail in the next chapter.

ACTUAL ENTITIES, CONCRESCENCE, AND PAN-EXPERIENTALISM

It should be evident that Whitehead's epistemology is connected to a view of reality that is much different from that of scientific materialism. Instead of a static view of reality thought to be composed of bits of brute matter, Whitehead argues that reality is constituted by events, or what he calls "actual occasions" or "actual events." These entities are brief pulses of creative activity that last but a moment. The process in which an actual entity becomes itself is called a "concrescence," thereby suggesting that it amounts to some sort of growth or "coming together." It literally means "becoming concrete." "'Concrescence' is the name for the process in which the universe of many things acquires an individual unity in a determinate relegation of each item of the 'many' to its subordination in the constitution of the novel 'one'" (*PR*, 211). What concresces and comes together within an actual entity is the entire past universe. An actual entity is a creative unification of the past into a single point of satisfaction. It is the process in which the "many become one and are increased by one" (*PR*, 21). Reality "is in each moment something dynamically and creatively alive, something constantly developing in reaction to what has been and to what might be."[18] Reality, for Whitehead, is this process.

Key here is that Whitehead is putting forward a theory of "pan-psychism," or what has been better called "pan-experientialism."[19] In contrast to the lifeless and disenchanted view of nature found in scientific materialism, Whitehead argues that all entities in the world have some level of experience. There is no dualism between experiencing entities and nonexperiencing entities, as there is in, for example, Descartes's dualism between minds and bodies. Not only do all actual entities have experience, but they also exhibit a degree of purposive behavior. An actual entity is made up of its prehensions, beginning with the massive influx of prehensions that constitute the past world. The form of definiteness displayed by an actual entity is due to the way in which these prehensions are unified. This unification is governed by what Whitehead calls the "subjective aim."

This is not the place to give an exposition of Whitehead's defense of this position, but we can note that much of recent science lends credence to Whitehead's pan-experientalism. For example, purposive behavior has been detected in bacteria and even DNA.[20] It should also be mentioned that pan-experientalism is not to be confused with the position that attributes *consciousness* to all actual entities. Consciousness and experience are not the same thing. Consciousness, Whitehead says, presupposes experience.

Although we may be well aware of the many difficulties of scientific materialism or other theories of "substance," it seems so obvious that our experience of the world involves things or objects that have endurance. For Whitehead, these enduring things, such as rocks or even electrons, are actually enduring structures of "momentary events in which the same form is repeated again and again."[21] Enduring objects are really, as Frederick Ferre describes, "vibrations or pulsations of energy."[22]

All of this involves a very complex elaboration; what is important for our purposes is that we understand that Whitehead's view of nature differs from that of the view in scientific materialism in that it is constituted by actual entities that have intrinsic value and exhibit purposive behavior. "Nature is," Whitehead says, "full-blooded. Real facts are happening" (*MT*, 144). The differences amount to a stance that states that something is going on in the world and that the constituents of the world are contributing to these happenings. Thus, Whitehead is not going to have a problem with the sort of other-worldliness that worried Nietzsche.

NOTES

1. It is largely with *Science and the Modern World*, written in 1925, that the concerns of Whitehead's published works broaden from concerns with mathematics, science, and the philosophy of science to philosophy in general and its influence on culture at large.

2. Whitehead was optimistic that developments in physics and biology were beginning to challenge the coherence and explanatory efficacy of the dominant worldview. But despite these advances, he noticed that public discourse was lagging behind and that many of the assumptions of materialism (the worldview in question) were firmly embedded in cultural institutions. These assumptions, he writes, "dominate the marketplace, the playgrounds, the law courts, and *in fact the whole sociological intercourse of mankind*" (*MT*, 130; emphasis added).

3. This definition of life is a bit more inclusive than the one he gives in *Adventures of Ideas*, in which he regards the essence of life as the "teleological introduction of novelty" (*AI*, 207). Here, life is limited to those entities that have a high enough grade of mentality to introduce significant novelty. In the definition given in *Modes of Thought*, "life" is extended to all individual actual entities because subjectivity and the enjoyment of emotion are characteristic of all actual entities.

4. A good discussion that sustains Whitehead's view concerning scientific materialism's theological heritage can be found in John Hedley Brooke's *Science and Religion: Some Historical Perspectives* (Cambridge: Cambridge University Press, 1991), 52–81.

5. Whitehead cites the following sentence in a letter from Newton to Richard Bentley: "When I wrote my treatise about our system, I had an eye upon such principles as might work with considering men for the belief of a Deity" (*PR*, 93).

6. See David Ray Griffin, *God and Religion in the Postmodern World: Essays in Postmodern Theology* (Albany: State University of New York Press, 1989), 84.

7. David Ray Griffin, "Introduction: The Reenchantment of Science," in *The Reenchantment of Science*, ed. David Ray Griffin (Albany: State University of New York Press, 1988), 2.

8. Darwin was at great pains to explain the use of the tale of a male peacock. At first glance, it appears to have no use. Darwin concluded that it survived because female peacocks preferred the males with the best ornamentation. He, in other words, supplemented the category of "natural selection" with that of "sexual selection," giving aesthetic values a real role to play. The inclusion of choice generated problems for those Darwinians who were more attached to a strictly mechanistic approach. Beginning with Wallace, sometime after 1871, the idea of female choice was rejected. See Helena

Cronin, *The Ant and the Peacock: Altruism and Sexual Selection From Darwin to Today* (Cambridge: Cambridge University Press, 1991), 123. This was pointed out to me by David Griffin.

9. David Hume, *A Treatise Concerning Human Nature*, ed. L. A Selby-Bigge (Oxford: Clarendon, 1951), Book I, Part IV, section 6.

10. Whitehead would agree with Hume that human beings are composed of "prehensions." But for Whitehead, human beings are a self-determining unification of their prehensions. They are not merely a bundle of impressions. Furthermore, Whitehead is able to defend the idea of personal identity through time. Like Hume, he denies the idea that the soul or mind is a numerically self-identical substance (*AI*, 186). Unlike Hume, he can account for personal identity by linking the past to the present through perception in the mode of causal efficacy. See David Griffin, *Unsnarling the World-Knot: Consciousness, Freedom, and the Mind-Body Problem* (Berkeley: University of California Press, 1998), 133–34. For a good discussion of Whitehead's view of the human soul, see John Cobb, *A Christian Natural Theology* (Philadelphia: Westminster, 1965), 47–91.

11. For example, in eye surgery, although the eyes of the patient are opened, the patient cannot see. This temporary blindness is not induced by inserting a sort of microscopic, opaque screen between the mind and the eye. Rather, it is achieved by anesthetizing the optic nerve, thus inhibiting the nerve from *feeling*.

12. The expression "direct perception" could be somewhat misleading, because Whitehead does not mean to suggest that this aspect of experience is necessarily conscious experience. He usually uses the term *prehension* to avoid the connotation that experience must always and only be conscious sense-perception. In *Science and the Modern World*, Whitehead writes, "The word *perceive* is, in our common usage, shot through and through with the notion of cognitive apprehension. . . . I will use the word *prehension* for *uncognitive apprehension*: by this I mean apprehension which may or may not be cognitive" (*SMW*, 69).

13. Although this is a complicated issue, it needs to be said here that Whitehead's epistemology is not a naïve realism. Conscious experience is not a simple and direct awareness of what is immediately given to the perceiver from without. Consciousness is the penultimate stage in an occasion of experience. For Whitehead, consciousness comes after much of the original data of experience has been sifted, sorted, and interpreted.

14. Thomas Wolfe, *Look Homeward Angel* (New York: Modern Library, 1934), 3.

15. Christopher Lasch finds the loss of a connection to the past to be one of the primary causes of a culture of narcissism. He writes, "To live for the moment is the prevailing passion—to live for yourself, not for your predecessors or posterity. We are fast losing the sense of historical continuity, the

sense of belonging to a succession of generations originating in the past and stretching into the future." *The Culture of Narcissism: American Life in an Age of Diminishing Expectations* (New York: Norton, 1979), 5.

16. The latter sentence of this passage is a quotation from Shakespeare's *A Midsummer's Night Dream*. Whitehead's interest in it is evidently sparked from the fact that the theme of much of the play is the role of imagination, fantasy, and illusion.

17. Griffin, *Unsnarling the World-Knot,* 140.

18. Thomas Hosinski, *Stubborn Fact and Creative Advance: An Introduction to the Metaphysics of Alfred North Whitehead* (Lanham, Md.: Rowman & Littlefield, 1993), 23.

19. See Griffin, *Unsnarling the World-Knot,* 78.

20. For a series of essays that discusses Whitehead's philosophy in relation to modern science, see *The Reenchantment of Science: Postmodern Proposals.*

21. Griffin, *God and Religion in the Postmodern World,* 64.

22. Frederick Ferre, *Being and Value: Toward a Constructive Postmodern Metaphysics* (Albany: State University of New York Press, 1996), 262.

8

Whitehead's View of God and the Religious Life

In the previous chapter, I discussed Whitehead's criticism of the dominant worldview of scientific materialism, paying particular attention to the way in which it viewed the natural world as a lifeless, disenchanted place where human aesthetic and ethical intuitions have no ontological standing. In its place, Whitehead offers a view of the world that is dynamically alive, and is constituted by entities that have intrinsic value. In this chapter, I engage in a more explicit discussion of Whitehead's account of religious experience and his doctrine of God. Along with my exposition, I want to show that Whitehead's doctrine of God and the religious life it fosters avoids much of Nietzsche's criticism of the Christian doctrine of God. Whitehead begins the last chapter of *Process and Reality* asking whether religion must always be antithetical to the value of immediate experience (*PR*, 342). What follows in the final pages of his book is a doctrine of God that attempts to answer no. His doctrine of God is, I suggest, an answer to the following "prophecy." "I hazard the prophecy that that religion will conquer which can render clear to popular understanding some eternal greatness incarnate in the passage of temporal fact" (*AI*, 33).

WHITEHEAD'S ACCOUNT OF RELIGIOUS EXPERIENCE

In a well-known passage, Whitehead writes that "religion is what the individual does with his own solitariness" (*RM*, 16). Part of what this means is that the religious life begins with the experience of the fact that one is an individual human being, "consciously alone with itself, for its own sake" (*RM*, 16).[1] This realization of individuality is an awareness that despite our traditions, cultures, histories, families, and the like, each human being is an entity that is not wholly determined by these and other forces. We have the capacity for freedom and disengagement. The great religions of the world, Whitehead writes, all bear witness to this realization of individual solitude. "The great religious conceptions which haunt the imaginations of civilized mankind are scenes of solitariness: Prometheus chained to his rock, Mahomet brooding in the desert, the meditations of the Buddha, the solitary Man on the Cross" (*RM*, 19–20). And as Donald Crosby writes:

> The vise-grip of tradition upon them will be broken, and they will no longer have the sense of being at the mercy of arbitrary power. They will be thrown upon their own resources . . . [and] there will emerge, phoenix-like, the awesome realization that each man is a solitary being, unique to himself, an irreducible focus and source of freedom and value.[2]

Religion begins with the experience of self-worth and self-value.

The experience of individual value and solitude is neither a solipsistic nor narcissistic experience of being the only thing that exists or is of importance. Rather, it is the experience of being an individual within a greater totality.[3] "The world is a scene of solitariness in community" (*RM*, 88). Along with the feeling of solitude, a moment of religious experience, according to Whitehead, is composed of two other concepts. They are the "value of the diverse individuals of the world for each other" and "the value of the objective world which is a community derivative from the interrelations of its component individuals" (*RM*, 59). Therefore, the experience of individual solitude "broadens into the concept of the world as a realm of adjusted values" (*RM*, 59). There is the realization of being an individual that is part of a greater whole (which is itself constituted by other intrinsically valuable entities) and that this whole, with its other individuals, is important for the well-being of the individual. "Actuality is the self-enjoyment of importance. But this self-enjoyment has the character of the self-enjoyment of others melting into the enjoyment of one self" (*MT*, 118). Religious experience leads to a feeling of what Whitehead calls "world-loyalty" (*RM*, 60).

We can see that religious experience is made possible by an openness to perception in the mode of causal efficacy. This openness is the basis of Whitehead's respect for the Romantic poets and their reaction against scientific materialism. It is through perception in the mode of causal efficacy that we experience the feeling of belonging to the world at large. Perception in the mode of causal efficacy is "the perception of the pressure from a world of things with characters in their own right, characters mysteriously moulding our own natures" (*S*, 44). We come to understand ourselves as internally related to the world. Perception in the mode of causal efficacy is the root of our feelings of sympathy.

> The primitive form of physical experience is emotional—blind emotion—received as felt elsewhere in another occasion and conformally appropriated as a subjective passion. In the language appropriate to the higher stages of experience, the primitive element is *sympathy*, that is, feeling the feeling *in* another and feeling conformally *with* another. (*PR*, 162)

Whitehead thinks that this fact of experience should lead us to a realization of the value of all that the world includes. "At the basis of our existence is the sense of worth" (*MT*, 109). The doctrine of perception in the mode of causal efficacy allows Whitehead to show that emotions and nonsensory feelings are at the root of experience. Respect for other human beings and the world at large arises as the result of the cultivation of these feelings of genuine sympathy. They give way to the idea that "we have no right to deface the value experience which is the very essence of the universe" (*MT*, 111). Imagining the subtle beauty of a single flower in an uninhabited forest, we realize that within the totality are innumerable instances of beauty and value that escape our purview.

> When we survey nature and think however flitting and superficial has been the animal enjoyment of its wonders, and when we realize how incapable the separate cells and pulsations of each flower are of enjoying the total effect—then our sense of the value of the details for the totality dawns upon our consciousness. (*MT*, 120)

This aesthetic experience of the totality of the world at large is understood religiously by Whitehead in that it is, he says, the intuition of holiness (*MT*, 120).

WHITEHEAD'S DOCTRINE OF GOD

We have discussed Whitehead's view of religious experience with little reference to the idea of God. One of the differences between religion and science is that the religious person is not content merely to justify his or her beliefs on their pragmatic benefits or "cash-value." Whitehead writes that unlike religion, science can "leave its metaphysics implicit and retire behind our belief in the pragmatic value of its general dogma" (*RM*, 85). Religion must penetrate further, for it is the desire of the religious person that "the facts of existence should find their justification in the nature of existence" (*RM*, 85). The religious person seeks to know that his or her experiences of value and world loyalty have some basis that is deeper than mere pragmatics; one wants to know that their experiences and practices are in accord with the way reality really is. We have seen how Whitehead's metaphysics and epistemology provide the justification for giving aesthetic and ethical experience some ontological footing. But we have not yet shown how Whitehead's metaphysics implies a theistic understanding of reality.

Whitehead's understanding of the nature of reality requires a divine principle, thus affirming that one's religious intuitions are supported by the nature of existence.

> The order of the world is no accident. There is nothing actual which could be actual without some measure of order. The religious insight is the grasp of this truth: . . . . *that the universe exhibits a creativity with infinite freedom, and a realm of forms with infinite possibilities; but that this creativity and these forms are together impotent to achieve actuality apart from the completed ideal harmony, which is God.* (*RM*, 119–120; emphasis added)

This passage describes two factors in our conception of reality that require the idea of God. Reality, as Whitehead understands it, is a process of diverse actual occasions, each arising out of the past as they come to be, unifying this past in a particular way, achieving a form of definiteness, and passing away. Reality is a continual process in which the "many become one and are increased by one." For any moment of reality or actuality to exist, there must be a realm of potential possibilities. "We conceive actuality as in essential relation to an unfathomable possibility" (*SMW*, 174). What something is, because it is finite, always involves a relation to other possibilities, to that which it is not. "Every actual occasion is a limitation imposed on possibility" (*SMW*, 174). To explain reality, there must be some factor in the universe that houses these possibilities.

In addition to the need for a realm of possibilities, we need to be able to explain that within the universe there is a drive toward novelty and, in particular, that there is an evolutionary progress. Whitehead writes that the long course of history is witness to an upward evolutionary development toward organisms with greater and greater complexity in structural organization. Quite unlike neo-Darwinian evolutionary theory, Whitehead holds that this upward development is due to some inherent teleology within the universe. Nature, Whitehead thinks, is obviously doing something other than producing species with greater and greater capacities for simple survival. If survival were the only criterion for success, then human beings would be quite near the bottom of the list. "The art of persistence is to be dead. Only inorganic things persist for great lengths of time. A rock survives for eight hundred million years . . . a man . . . about fifty or one hundred years" (*FR*, 4–5).

Rather, evolutionary history is witness to a growth in species that have more complex schemes of organization and a greater capacity for mental functioning.[4] "The whole point of the modern doctrine is the evolution of the complex organisms from antecedent states of less complex organisms" (*SMW*, 107). Scientific materialism's version of evolution is unable to explain this phenomenon.

> The fact that organic species have been produced from inorganic distributions of matter, and the fact that in the lapse of time organic species of higher and higher types have evolved are not in the least explained by any doctrine of adaptations to the environment, or of struggle. (*FR*, 7)

There is little correlation between higher organisms showing an increase in mentality and the ability for survival.

In contrast to the dominant ideas of neo-Darwinism, Whitehead argues that many of the activities of organisms are directed by purposes. He thinks this is quite obvious. Animals, he says, have "progressively undertaken the task of adapting the environment" (*FR*, 7), which is to say that it is evident that there are many actions that are motivated by foresight, aim, and purpose. "There is clear evidence that certain operations of certain bodies depend upon the foresight of an end and the purpose to attain it" (*FR*, 16). Purpose, aim, and foresight exist on both the microcosmic level of individual acts and the macrocosmic level of the world as a whole.

Whitehead holds that the general end, aim, or purpose of all activity in the universe is an "increase in value." "The problem of evolution is the development of enduring harmonies of enduring shapes of value, which merge into higher attainments of things beyond themselves" (*SMW*, 94). Therefore, quite unlike proponents of neo-Darwinism, Whitehead defends the idea that there is evolutionary progress in terms of higher forms of organisms that have a greater capacity for mental functioning. It is with this capacity for mental functioning that greater values are realized. Whitehead describes this increase of value in aesthetic terms. The "teleology of the Universe is," he writes, "directed to the production of beauty" (*AI*, 265). The course of evolutionary history is being driven by the entertainment of various ideals. Therefore, some factor in the universe must be able to account for these ideals. For Whitehead, the factor in the universe that accounts for the realm of possibility and the presence of ideals is God. Cobb and Griffin write, "In sum, God is that factor in the universe which establishes what-is-not as relevant to what-is, and lures the world toward new forms of realization."[5]

For Whitehead, the purpose of the universe is the creation of novel beauty. Unlike neo-Darwinian evolutionary theory, Whitehead holds that the cosmos is being directed by a power other than "natural selection." This *telos* and the advance into new forms of beauty is made possible by the presence of God in the universe. More specifically, the purpose of the universe is the actualization of the ideals in the "primordial nature" of God. God is the Eros of the universe, urging it toward the "realization of ideal perfection" (*AI*, 275).

The meaning of human life (and what it means to be religious) is to participate in God's purpose. This participation is twofold. First, as we discussed, one can be open to, and receptive of, the world, enjoying the fact that one lives in a world in which something is going on. We can appreciate the fact that we live in a universe, not where the "molecules blindly run" (*SMW*, 77–78) but where there is a drive toward some ideal (*MT*, 120). There is the gift of "being an actuality in a world of actualities" (*MT*, 120). Second, for Whitehead, the purpose of human existence is more than passive observation or feeling. Human beings are to participate in God's purpose by becoming embodiments of God's values. In other words, human beings are to be involved in the creation of beauty by living lives of creativity.

Before going further, we can address a criticism that arises from the perspective of Nietzsche. One of the great consequences of the death of God is that we must now deny that the universe is heading toward some ultimate goal or final end. Nietzsche claims that the belief in this final end was another one of the ways in which the reality of Becoming was denied. Whitehead's advocation of a teleological universe seems to put him at odds with Nietzsche. While this is a real difference, Whitehead's understanding of this purpose does not amount to a denial of the reality of Becoming. Whitehead is not suggesting that the universe is moving toward some final point at which, when reached, the universe will stop. "The immensity of the world negatives the belief that any state of order can be established that beyond it there can be no progress" (*PR*, 111). Whitehead's reason for rejecting this type of teleology stems from his rejection of the Platonic idea of permanence. Process, change, and becoming are not characteristics of a less than eminent reality. *They are the categories of reality.* Belief in the possibility of the static maintenance of perfection is behind the belief that the world is moving towards some thing static. Whitehead says that Tennyson's phrase "one far-off divine event/To which the whole creation moves" presents a "fallacious conception of the universe" (*PR*, 111). Furthermore, because the telos of the universe is toward aesthetic values there can be no ultimate, unsurpassable achievement of beauty. As Hartshorne remarks, "Aesthetic value is the most concrete form of value. Everything can contribute to and increase it. *An absolute maximum of beauty is a meaningless idea.*"[6] Because only a finite actuality can be deemed beautiful, all such instances are limited. But this limitation is not a defect, as if finitude were an imperfection. "Absolute beauty is a will-o-the-wisp, the search for which has misled multitudes."[7] Whitehead's own understanding of cosmic purpose does not make becoming unreal.

God's Primordial Nature

> I am inside the thunder as well as the lightning. I am inside all blasts of passion, for it is there that I rejuvenate myself. . . . I immersed myself in whatever I did. I was and I was not my world. I was the impulse that lived in it; and the world inhabited by my soul, went its own way.
>
> —*Franco Ferrucci*, The Life of God (as Told by Himself)

As I said, the purpose of the universe is the production of novel beauty. In particular, the purpose of the universe is to become the realization of God's own vision of beauty. This vision exists in what Whitehead calls God's "primordial nature." The primordial nature is that aspect of God that fulfills the need for a realm of potentials. It is "the unlimited conceptual realization of the absolute wealth of potentiality" (*PR*, 343). In other words, God prehends, as conceptual ideals, the entire wealth of possibility for the universe. Whitehead calls these possibilities "eternal objects." They are the "pure potentials of the universe" (*PR*, 149).

Eternal objects, then, are timeless, unembodied, and infinite. In some respects, they resemble Plato's forms. Although these eternal objects are, in themselves, without intrinsic value, they have what can be called "inherent value" in the sense that they *would* have value if realized within certain concrete situations. For example, the color red is neither good nor bad, beautiful nor ugly. But within certain events it may be one or the other. In a sunset, the color red might be deemed beautiful, but the sight of blood on a loved one will probably produce a very different reaction. But, God's primordial nature is more than a mere assemblage of these eternal objects. In addition, there is an assessment of the value of eternal objects within concrete situations. In this way, God's prehension of these possibilities is neither unbiased nor neutral. The primordial nature also involves "an order in the relevance of eternal objects" (*PR*, 344). This aspect of the primordial nature of God is God's vision for how things *ought* to be within particular situations.

God's goal is to realize this vision in the world. To bring it about, God attempts to persuade or lure the actual entities of the world toward the realization of the particular form of definiteness God desires. In every occasion of experience there is a prehension of God's primordial nature. Whitehead calls this prehension the "initial aim." It provides the ideal by which the concrescing actual entity can best contribute to the purpose of the universe, which is the production of novel beauty. "In this function . . . God is the organ of novelty, aiming at intensification" (*PR*, 64). Although these ideals are nonsensuous, they are prehended. It might seem that if God is directing the course of the universe by supplying the initial aim, Whitehead's understanding of God's power is coercive, which, as we saw earlier, is something Whitehead wanted to avoid. This is not the case, as all actual entities have a degree of self-determination, thus allowing them the freedom to deviate from God's aim.

The presence of God's initial aim in each actual occasion accounts for the experience of ideals. "There are experiences of ideals—of ideals entertained, of ideals aimed at, of ideals achieved, of ideals defaced. This is the experience of the deity of the universe" (*MT*, 103). Unlike Hume, Whitehead states that these ideals are not mere "customs." As a vision of the way things ought to be, God's primordial nature is a "principle of rightness" (*RM*, 61).

Some of this talk about a "perfect world" and a vision of the way things *ought* to be is reminiscent of the Socratic-Platonism and Christianity that are susceptible to Nietzsche's criticism that the True World of Being is a concept that denigrates the finite World of Becoming because it stands in judgment of it. Before quickly identifying Whitehead's views with those criticized by Nietzsche, however, we should make note of some crucial differences. Whitehead avoids the nihilistic and otherwordly tendencies of Plato's notion of the Forms. The fact that God is primordial and that the eternal objects are timeless should, by no means, be used to advance the idea that they have the quality of eminence. With regard to the primordial nature of God, Whitehead says, "But, as primordial, so far is he from 'eminent reality,' that in this abstraction he is deficiently actual" (*PR*, 343). The primordial nature of God is deficient in the sense that what is envisioned and the envisaging itself lack actuality. According to Whitehead's ontological principle, that which is really real is not the unembodied eternal objects but the actual entities that embody such forms. With regard to the eternal objects, they are not actual. They do not exist in their own right and have no intrinsic value. Using the word *value* in place of *eternal object*, Whitehead writes. "The status of the World of Value is that of an abstraction requiring, for the completion of its concrete reality, the factuality of Finite Activity" (IMM, 100).

Whereas Plato would say *the particular is lacking by virtue of its finitude*, Whitehead would go the other way, saying that *the universal is lacking by virtue of its infinitude*. What is permanent, unembodied, and eternal is lacking. It lacks actuality. The primordial nature of God is an eternal permanence that requires "fluency as its completion" (*PR*, 347). The mere conceptual envisagement of eternal objects or beautiful ideas is not enough for God. What God desires is for the conceptual to become actual, for the eternal to become finite. "We must conceive the Divine Eros as the active entertainment of all ideals, with the urge to their finite realization, each in its due season. *Although it is part of God's nature to be eternal, what is purely eternal or timeless lacks actuality"* (*AI*, 277; emphasis added). To be actual is to be embodied and to be embodied is to be finite, fluid, and temporal. Thus, for Whitehead, God's primordial nature does not provide us with a vision of an immortal and perfect world that is superior to this world. That which is eternal and infinite is lacking in actuality. For Whitehead, God does not prefer the vision of the perfect world in the primordial nature to the actual world. This vision, for God, is deficient in its lack of actuality, which means its lack of finitude. Its deficiency is due precisely to the fact that it is unembodied and infinite.

For Nietzsche, one of the problems with the True World of Being is that it makes finitude the problem. It states that the finite lacks perfection and authenticity because it is finite. Given Whitehead's criticism of the Platonic notion of permanence and the static fallacy, we can see that he would agree with Nietzsche's criticism. Although God's primordial nature does provide the comforting thought that there is a vision of perfection, it is not the vision Nietzsche identified as decadent and nihilistic. Plato's endorsement of the superiority of the eternal, infinite, and unembodied is due to the mistaken tendency of "sensitive people, when they experience some factor of value on its noblest side, to feel that they are enjoying some ultimate essence of the Universe, and that therefore its existence must include an absolute independence of all inferior types" (IMM, 100). The mistake these "sensitive people" make in their experience of value is to think it would be possible to experience some value or another in an unembodied, eternal, and unsurpassable manner. But such a value would be a mere abstraction, lacking actuality. The primordial nature of God, with its infinite, nondecaying, and unconditioned eternal objects, does not judge this world as inferior because it is composed of Socrates' doomed entities that wander between the poles of generation and decay. Therefore, although the primordial nature of God can serve as a bar of judgment, it is not the judgment that the world of Becoming is inferior because it is finite. Unlike Leibniz, Whitehead's cosmology does not have the category of "metaphysical evil," which is the alleged evil of being a finite actuality.[8] Whitehead's view of the relation between eternal objects or universals and particular actual entities is similar to Goethe's:

There is a great difference between a poet seeking the particular for the universal, and seeing the universal in the particular. The former gives rise to Allegory, where the particular serves only as an instance or example of the general; but the other is the true nature of Poetry. . . . If a man grasps the particular vividly he also grasps the general.[9]

For Whitehead, the world is not merely an allegory of the mind of God. It is the actualization of the universal within particular actual entities.

All of this is quite startling because we are beginning to see that Whitehead's God is a God with desires, appetites, and needs. This is hardly the God Nietzsche described as "castrated" (*A*, 16). Nor is it a God that could endorse a wholesale rejection of the passions. Whitehead often described God's primordial nature as the "primordial appetition." And in *Adventures of Ideas*, Whitehead largely shied away from the word "God," choosing instead to call God the "Eros of the Universe" (*AI*, 11). Deep within the nature of God looms the desire to create and actualize what is, in the beginning, only a conceptual ideal. This is God's desire for novelty. God wants to pour out into the world. Whitehead is reported as saying that God "is both constructive and destructive, i.e., is concerned to get rid of repetition, and to have new orders and entities built up."[10] As we will see, a God with desires, aesthetic tastes, and passion would hardly expect otherwise of its creatures. Whereas Nietzsche complained that Christianity encouraged an "unselfing" of the human being and an overall weakening of human personality, Whitehead's God supports a religiosity that is worldly, gives value to the individual, and encourages various pursuits *in the world.*

The Immediate Harvest of Value

But after all, there must be some immediate harvest. The good of the Universe cannot lie in indefinite postponement.

—*Alfred North Whitehead*, Adventures of Ideas

From what has been said so far, we can draw an important point that speaks to Nietzsche's concern that the idea of God defers the fulfillment of human existence to a "place" outside the world of Becoming. While Nietzsche was keen to show that the meaning of existence promised by Christianity comes only at the end of life, Whitehead

maintains that the "subjective aim," or purpose, of God is the realization of intrinsically valuable experience *in* the world. "God's purpose
in the creative advance is the evocation of intensities" (*PR*, 105).
God's desire that values in the primordial nature become realized in
the actual world returns a sense of meaningfulness to the historical
process.[11] "The purpose of God is the attainment of value in the temporal world" (*RM*, 100). Thus, the quality of existence is to be adjudicated by the success or failure of this goal. "The Day of Judgment is
an important notion: but that Day is always with us" (*AI*, 269).

This understanding of God's purpose is quite different than that
found in the "Christian-moral" interpretation criticized by Nietzsche.
Whitehead's deity does not require its believers to forsake the present. As I stated earlier and will discuss in more detail later, God provides each actual occasion with an "initial aim," which is God's vision of how that occasion can best reach the highest form of
intensity.

Given that Whitehead understands religious experience as the experience of self-value, we can see that his account differs from the
growing tendency of Western thought toward an "unselfing" of human individuality that Nietzsche saw associated with the growth of
Christian values and ideals. Whitehead contrasts his view of religious experience, with its emphasis on solitude and self-value, with
earlier forms of religious experience as manifested in "communal religion."[12] In communal religion, God is, Whitehead says, something
of an "enemy" (*RM*, 16–17), by which he means that God's interests
are not aligned with human interests. God is understood as a power
that is to be feared and placated. For this reason, communal religion
is more authoritarian, for it is constantly involved in the effort to
please God so that God will not be angered. Everything depends on
the will of God; one's well-being is dependent on an allegiance to
this will. "In a communal religion you study the will of God in order
that He may preserve you" (*RM*, 41). Communal religion, Crosby
writes commenting on Whitehead's view, "distrusts individual honesty, initiative, and self-discovery in its anxiety not to let anything
disturb the tenuous and fragile relationship it has established with
the gods."[13] Communal religion breeds conformity to the group,
teaching human beings to define themselves only in relation to the
community. In Whitehead's own view of religious experience, God
is understood as the "companion" (*RM*, 17). God's interests are in

promoting the interests of individuals. For Whitehead, the religious life does not involve a weakening or "unselfing" of the human being. Rather, God, as the companion, is concerned with the achievement of value in the world. The economy of this view of the religious life is *not* the simple exchange of the self and its interests for something outside the self. This is not to say, however, that Whitehead's religion involves a simple egoism or a simple valorization of the present moment at the expense of either others or the future. Rather, it is his view that the interests of an individual need not be seen as in conflict with the interest of the greater whole and a concern for future occasions. In fact, such concerns can add to the value of the present. "For the inevitable anticipation adds to the present a qualitative element which profoundly affects its whole qualitative harmony" (*AI*, 269).

At Home in the World and the Importance of Openness

> I am now pleading that our whole experience is composed out of our relationships to the rest of things, and of the formation of new relationships constitutive of things to come.
>
> —*Alfred North Whitehead*, Modes of Thought

> The body widens, and people are welcomed into it, many at a time. This must be what happens when we learn to be generous.
>
> —*Stephen Dunn*, The Snowmass Cycle

For God to succeed in persuading the world toward higher forms of intensities of experience, actual entities in the world must be directed into the world of relationality. In other words, to be religious, to participate in God's purpose, is to be unlike the ascetic priest criticized by Nietzsche for withdrawing from the world and its enticements. For Nietzsche, the call of Christianity (as well as the dominant trend of Western thought) is to "cease all intercourse with earthly things" (*A*, 14) and to maintain a defensive and isolated stance against the world. Because Whitehead takes God's aim to be the realization of value in the world, human beings who are committed to this God can feel at home in the world. The world is the domain in which God seeks to realize the vision of the primordial nature. As participants in God's purpose, we are to seek to maximize our involvement in the world. If we do not feel at home in the world, life becomes either a project of ascetic withdrawal or a search for various forms of anesthetic comfort. In Nietzsche's terms, we must choose between the life of the "priest" and that of the "last man." Common to the response of the last man and the priest is the desire to limit or eliminate the degree of influence of those factors outside the self.

What I would like to focus on in this section is how Whitehead's theistic philosophy provides the basis for an *antiascetic anthropology*. Whitehead's anthropology maintains that the economy between the human being and the world is a constant flow between the two. The world flows into the person, and the person flows back into the world. To show that this is the case, I need to elaborate our discussion of Whitehead's theory of concrescence.

An actual entity is a creative unification of the past into a single point of satisfaction. It is the process in which the "many become one." The process of concrescence, which is the life of an occasion of experience, has two main stages or phases: the physical pole and the mental pole.

In the first phase, the physical pole or the phase of "physical" or "conformal feelings," the entire past universe "enters into the constitution of the entity in question" (*PR*, 152). It is a phase of "pure reception" (*PR*, 212). This phase is composed of "perception in the mode of causal efficacy." Every entity begins by prehending everything that has occurred in the past. Included in this series of prehensions is a feeling of what Whitehead calls the "initial aim." This aim is a "hybrid physical prehension" of God's primordial nature. It is a prehension of a possibility for how the concrescing entity can best become, given the situation.

Following this massive influx of given data, the mental pole begins. The actual entity begins to sort through its "physical prehensions," attempting to bring them together, to become one. In other words, the actual entity reacts to what it has been given. "The physical inheritance is essentially accompanied by a conceptual reaction" (*PR*, 108). This reaction is governed by what Whitehead calls the "subjective aim," which is an adaptation of God's initial aim. In this phase, the actual entity decides what it will do with the data, creating itself out of the given. Whereas the physical pole can be equated with efficient causation, the mental pole involves final causation. In the majority of cases, as with the actual entities that make up a rock, the actual entity merely reiterates the immediate past. In more complex actual entities, those that have a higher grade of mentality, more activity is found in the mental pole. An actual entity may draw the universe together in a new way, thus introducing an element of novelty. When this occurs, it is often due to a conformity of the subjective aim to God's initial aim. "The novel hybrid feelings derived from God, with the derivative sympathetic conceptual valuations, are the foundations of progress" (*PR*, 247).

This process ends as the actual entity succeeds in drawing the past together into a single point of "satisfaction." When this occurs, the actual entity's subjectivity perishes, but the entity obtains "objective immortality" in that it is now part of the past, thereby exerting causal influence on entities to come.

Whitehead's theory of experience is extremely complex, and its elucidation is the major task of *Process and Reality*. What is important for our purposes is the essentially social nature of all actual entities. "There is no entity, not even God, which requires nothing but itself in order to exist. . . . Every entity is in its essence social and requires society in order to exist" (*RM*, 108). Whitehead's point involves more than the claim that we need the help of others to sustain our well-being. To say that "every entity is in its essence social" means that all actual entities are *constituted* by their relations. They are internally related to all others. "An actual entity *is* present in other actual entities" (*PR*, 50). This is Whitehead's "principle of relativity." All actual entities emerge out of the world and flow back into the world.

The essential relatedness of all actual entities is not only a metaphysical characteristic. It has ethical and aesthetic significance as well. The richness or quality of human life is greatly affected by, as John Cobb writes, "the variety and quality of entities [the self] encounters and in its own willingness and ability to be open to what they can contribute."[14] The last part of Cobb's point is especially important. If one is to flourish, develop, and live abundantly, one must seek and be open to the idea that something other than the self contributes to one's well-being. For Whitehead, a human being flourishes when a stance of open receptivity to the world is maintained. This receptivity increases the potential for the creation of beauty. As we saw, beauty "is the mutual adaptation of the several factors in an occasion of experience" (*AI*, 252). Beauty is achieved when several factors have been brought together in such a way that there is neither a discordant and vulgar clash of difference nor a homogenized uniformity. An object of beauty has "patterned contrasts." "All aesthetic experience is feeling arising out of the realization of contrast under identity" (*RM*, 115). For Whitehead, this is true at all levels, from electronic and atomic actual occasions, to the dominant occasions of human beings, to God's own experience.

The possibility for contrast is provided by the fact that within the physical pole is a massive diversity of various influences. The entire past world is impinging on the concrescing actual entity. Most of these influences are "negatively prehended," which means that they are simply not felt. "A negative prehension holds its datum as inoperative in the progressive concrescence of prehensions constituting the unity of the subject" (*PR*, 23–24). Although these negative prehensions are necessary, too many of them reduce the opportunities for beauty because they reduce the possibilities for contrast. But if an actual entity can preserve a variety of contrasts without letting them clash to the point of "aesthetic destruction," an occasion of experience can achieve a new level of depth and profundity. "The strength of experience in massiveness and in intensity, depends upon the substratum of detail being composed of significant individuals" (*AI*, 263). Marjorie Suchocki writes:

> The more influences allowed, the more novelty is called for. The "might be" comes into play as ways of integrating the many into unity come to the fore. . . . Consciousness, then, relies upon an openness to novelty and thus a prominence to the mental pole, a prominence that increases through the intensity of contrasts the occasion can sustain.[15]

Beauty is produced by an entity's "size." In an essay entitled "S-I-Z-E is the Measure," Bernard Loomer writes:

> By *size* I mean the stature of a person's soul, the range and depth of his love, his capacity for relationships. I mean the volume of life you can take into your being and still maintain your integrity and individuality. . . . I mean the power to sustain more complex and enriching tensions.[16]

As with Nietzsche, experience increases its capacity for profundity when one does not seek to repress the influence of various feelings. The experience of the last man is shallow and superficial because he no longer has any tensions. I think that one could insert Nietzsche's statement "the price of fruitfulness is to be rich in internal opposition" (*TI*, "Morality as Anti-Natural," 3) into a book by Whitehead without arousing the suspicion of Whitehead's most pedantic readers. For Whitehead, the religious life is not a search for a way out of this world, for an "improved" condition that has no tension. "Above and beyond all things, the religious life is not research after comfort" (*SMW*, 191). We are to maximize this tension to the degree that it does not result in "anarchy" or "aesthetic destruction."

In sum, an actual entity reaches greater heights of experience if it can successfully integrate a large number of contrasting influences. The more open an entity is and the more it allows itself to feel, the greater its experience. "The greatest enjoyment requires contrasts and contrasts of contrasts."[17] By eliminating influences, by closing itself off to the contributions of others, an actual occasion ends up as a trivial moment.

Creating Reality

The next question I would like to consider is whether Whitehead's theistic philosophy can support the life of playful creativity Nietzsche so admired in the child. The death of God, for Nietzsche, reveals an "open sea" in which we are free to create our own values, shaping reality how we may. With no preordained rules to follow, the child is free to play in, and experiment with, reality. In Whitehead's theistic philosophy, the possibilities for shaping and creating reality are present. Reality is not a static and fixed medium in which we live. It is, Whitehead says, plastic (*AI*, 42), meaning that it can be shaped. In fact, an occasion of experience is an instance of creativity in which reality has been shaped. The point of satisfaction is precisely how that actual entity chose to bring the past together. To be sure, the "plastic power" (as Nietzsche would call it) of most actual entities is slight. Most actual entities can only repeat the past. The actual entities of a rock are largely incapable of bringing the past together in new ways. But in actual entities that have a high grade of mental functioning—which means that they are significantly capable of intuiting, entertaining, and acting on alternative possibilities—there is a greater capacity for shaping and creating reality. For Whitehead, true novelty is possible because of the presence of God in the universe. New possibilities enter the world of actual occasions by means of God's primordial nature, which includes the realm of all eternal objects. Without these possibilities, there would only be a finite number of ways in which the past could be brought together.

One of the more interesting contributions of Whitehead's theory is that it breaks down the barriers between appearance and reality, on the one hand, and mentality and physicality, on the other. It provides a way for showing how our creations and ideas, however fanciful, can be woven into the fabric of reality. What occurs in the mental pole is passed on to the future in that it becomes part of the "given," part of the physical inheritance of future actual entities. "These antecedent appearances are part of the real functioning of the real actual world as it stands in the primary phase of the immediately present occasion" (*AI*, 212). In this way, Whitehead concludes, "there is an intimate, inextricable fusion of appearance with reality" (*AI*, 212).

At this point, one may make two objections. First, one could say that if novelty requires God's initial aim, the freedom of human beings and their capacity for creating their own realities seems severely limited. A couple of things can be said to this objection. In respect to human freedom in general, much of Whitehead's objection to the traditional doctrine of God and its ensuing mechanistic account of nature is made in defense of freedom. God is not the sole power in the universe. All actual entities have some degree of freedom. The initial aim is not a coercive force; it is only a suggestion. God, for Whitehead, can direct the universe only through persuasion. On Whitehead's account, it is possible to deviate from the initial aim.

We can add that Whitehead's doctrine of God actually provides more opportunities for novel creativity than Nietzsche's theory can. On Nietzsche's own admission and despite the fact that he says that the universe provides an infinite number of possible interpretations (*GS*, 374), the doctrine of eternal return, if it is seen as part of a cosmology, purports that there can only be a finite number of possibilities for creativity. If God is dead, the idea of eternal novelty loses support (*WP*, 1062; 1885). In his notebooks, Nietzsche insists that the amount of energy in the universe is finite. Therefore, he concludes, only a finite number of possible combinations exist. "It follows that, in the great dice game of existence, it must pass through a calculable number of combinations. In infinite time, every possible combination would at some time or another be realized" (*WP*, 1066; 1888). For Whitehead, the presence of God in each concrescing actual entity provides possibilities not necessarily present in the past. Thus, far from limiting or prohibiting the possibilities for novel creativity, God is the guarantee of such possibilities. God is the ground of freedom.

Another possible objection would be based on Nietzsche's contention that monotheism prohibits this sort of playfulness because if there is only one God, there is only one strict code of morality and one way of being authentic. We saw that Whitehead, like Nietzsche, criticizes the supernatural doctrine of God because it lends itself to a morality with absolutist and inflexible moral codes. So how does Whitehead's monotheism differ from the tradition in this respect? This question arose at a conference in 1983 devoted to an inquiry of the common themes between Whitehead's process thought and the psychology of Carl Jung and James Hillman. Hillman, as Griffin reports in his introduction to the published volume of conference papers, rejected monotheism because he thought it was incapable of supporting a "polytheistic psychology,"[18] a psychology that affirms a multitude of ways of being human. But, as Griffin argues, Whitehead's monotheism can be reconciled with Hillman's defense of pluralism. Whitehead's God is not directing the universe to a single ideal. "There is no perfection which is the infinitude of all perfections" (*AI*, 257). There is, as Griffin writes, "no One Right Way for all human beings."[19] Greatness, Whitehead writes, exists in a variety of contrasting styles of life.[20]

> There is a greatness in the lives of those who build up religious systems, a greatness in action, in idea and in self-subordination, embodied in instance after instance through centuries of growth. There is a greatness in the rebels who destroy such systems: they are the Titans who storm heaven, armed with passionate sincerity. (*PR*, 337–38)

Therefore, although Whitehead strongly defends the idea that there is an inherent drive or teleology directing the course of events, it differs significantly from the view that the universe is heading to some non-historical point at which only then things will reach authenticity. All of reality is not moving toward one event.

Up to this point, I have been describing Whitehead's view of the primordial nature of God and his idea that the "teleology of the Universe is the production of beauty" (*AI*, 265). For Whitehead, we can say that the meaning and purpose of human life is the experience and creation of beauty. Human beings can subscribe to the idea that they are involved in something important. The "basic expression" of experience is, Whitehead writes, "Have a care, here is something that matters!" (*MT*, 116). All of this means that human life in the world is valuable *because* of the world and *within* the world. Beauty is created and experienced by an open and affirmative stance in the world. Therefore, unlike the decadent and nihilistic value system of Western thought criticized by Nietzsche for giving otherworldly answers to the value of human life, Whitehead's value system is both theistic and "this-worldly."

Furthermore, it is based on *aesthetic* values. We saw in Nietzsche's first book, *The Birth of Tragedy*, that he concluded that the only way the world can be justified is as an aesthetic phenomenon. Although he later moved beyond much of what he said in *The Birth of Tragedy*, he still held to the idea that our justifications for the world and human life must be intrinsic to life in the world. Whitehead would not disagree with the claim that the justification for our lives and world is aesthetic, which is to say that it is the enjoyment of beauty that gives life meaning. "The real world," Whitehead writes, "is good when it is beautiful" (*AI*, 268). The supreme purpose of life, for Whitehead, is not to be moral (although this is important at the level of human life), nor is it to discover the truth (although this too is important). Truth and ethics matter because of the contributions they make to the creation of beauty. "Thus Beauty is left as the one aim which by its very nature is self-justifying" (*AI*, 266).

The Consequent Nature of God

Although a life of creating and experiencing beauty is intrinsically valuable, life in the world has a tragic quality to it. No matter how successful we are in our openness to, and creation of, beauty, one pressing and undeniable fact stands in the way. "Decay, Transition, Loss, Displacement belong to the essence of the Creative Advance" (*AI*, 286). The fact that the primary quality of reality is one of Becoming entails that "existence is entwined with pain, frustration, loss, tragedy" (*AI*, 286). Although it is true that our accomplishments achieve "objective immortality" in the world, meaning that they are passed on to future generations, this influence ultimately fades away. The "past fades," Whitehead says. This fact creates the ultimate problem:

> But objective immortality within the temporal world does not solve the problem set by the penetration of the finer religious intuition. 'Everlast-

ingness' has been lost; and 'everlastingness' is the content of that vision upon which the finer religions are built—the 'many' absorbed everlastingly in the final unity. (*PR*, 347)

When Nietzsche became aware of the problem of the loss of permanence or "everlastingness," he felt it was an unavoidable fact. For him, the losses associated with the death of God must be overcome within a world that is forever ephemeral. He seeks a solution that does not (at least explicitly) rely on a "metaphysical comfort" that reduces the tragic reality of life in the world of Becoming.

For Whitehead, the experience of perishing and the loss of everlastingness seeks an answer. We are left wondering whether our achievements and failures have any significance beyond the immediate fact. And, unlike Nietzsche, Whitehead thought the affirmation of human life in the world required that they do have significance. Cobb writes:

> If beauty is to be sought without ruthlessness, and if it is to be enjoyed without the poignant doubt of its worth, there must be an intuition that the worth of beauty exceeds its momentary enjoyment, that its attainment is self-justifying beyond the ability of reason to grasp its value.[21]

Whitehead's response to the losses involved in the passage of time is quite different from Nietzsche's answer. The problems caused by the tragic nature of existence and the loss of everlastingness are solved by what Whitehead calls the "consequent nature" of God.

If God exemplifies the same basic metaphysical principles as do the actualities of the world, as Whitehead insists, the actual entities of the world must be constitutive of God. The principle of relativity applies to God as well. God is, as Whitehead says, "incomplete" (*PR*, 345). The relative and fluid nature of God is part of God's "consequent nature." Just the name of this aspect of God suggests that the nature of God is a consequence of something other than God, so that God is not exclusively eternal and absolute. "There is a reaction of the world on God" (*PR*, 345).[22] The consequent nature is initiated by God's prehensions of the world.

Because of these prehensions, "perpetual perishing" and the incessant becoming of the world do not constitute the whole story. Whitehead writes that God "saves the world as it passes into the immediacy of his own life" (*PR*, 346). And again: "The consequent nature of God is the fluent world become 'everlasting' by its objective immediacy in

God" (*PR*, 347). Whatever occurs—be it in front of a television camera or in a closet—is retained forever in God's consequent nature. Whatever happens ultimately matters because it matters to, and is constitutive of, God's becoming. Achieved values are saved from loss because they live on in God.

But these prehensions are not merely "stored" in God, sitting passively. Rather, in God's consequent nature, the world, with its losses and evils, is *saved*.

> The wisdom of [God's] subjective aim prehends every actuality for what it can be in such a perfected system—its sufferings, its sorrows, its failures, its triumphs, its immediacies of joy—woven by rightness of feeling into the harmony of the universal feeling which is always immediate, always many, always one, always with novel advance, moving onward and never perishing. (*PR*, 346)

Just as every actual occasion has the potential of harmonizing a host of disorderly contrasts, so, too, has God, but with even greater capacity. With God, there are no negative prehensions. The entirety of the past world is harmonized in God. With the capacity to weave everything together into a harmony of extraordinary depth and breadth, God overcomes evil. "Suffering attains its end in a Harmony of Harmonies" (*AI*, 296).

By means of the consequent nature of God, one is granted the feeling of peace. For Whitehead, peace is an intuition of the efficacy of beauty and the reality of lasting permanence. Peace can create a feeling of trust and the removal of fear by providing one with the assurance that one's achievements have meaning beyond the immediate experience of intrinsic value. We can know that our achievements of value are efficacious and everlasting. The consequent nature of God is the assurance that our participation in the adventure of the creation of beauty is ultimately meaningful. It offers an answer to the anxiety of living in a world where perpetual perishing is an unavoidable fact. Moving us beyond fear, peace brings about a "removal of the stress of acquisitive feeling arising from the soul's preoccupation with itself" (*AI*, 285). In peace, one can "escape a restless egotism" (*AI*, 285) and cultivate a "world-loyalty." "It is a sense that fineness of achievement is, as it were, a key unlocking treasures that the narrow nature of things would keep remote. *There is thus involved a grasp of infinitude, an appeal beyond boundaries*" (*AI*, 285; emphasis added).

Although both contain the quality of trust, peace differs somewhat from Nietzsche's idea of *amor fati*. Nietzsche's concepts of *amor fati* and eternal return are attempts at affirming human life without any sort of metaphysical consolation or redemption from the fact that a reality of Becoming entails loss. "Becoming must appear justified at every moment. . . . The present must absolutely not be justified by reference to a future, nor the past by reference to the present" (*WP*, 708; 1888). The decisive feature of Nietzsche's Dionysian philosophy is "the affirmation of passing away *and destroying*." It is, he continues, "saying Yes to . . . *becoming*, along with a radical repudiation of the very concept of *being*" (*EH*, "The Birth of Tragedy," 3). To a Nietzschean, Whitehead seems ultimately to want more than a reality characterized by Becoming can provide. Whitehead insists that without the consequent nature of God and the assurance of some form of immortality for all of the accomplishments in the world, human existence is trivial. "The cry, 'Let us eat and drink, for tomorrow we die,' expresses the triviality of the merely finite" (*MT*, 79). To Nietzsche, Whitehead would have seemed like one who resorts to the concept of God only because life is not endurable in God's absence. "How many there are who still conclude 'life could not be endured if there were no God!' (or, as it is put among the idealists: 'life could not be endured if its foundations lacked an ethical significance')—therefore there *must* be a God" (*D*, 90). In the end, for Whitehead, the ability to affirm life in the world is attained by knowing that everything that occurs in the world is meaningful *because* it matters to God, who is everlasting. "The full solemnity of the world arises from the sense of positive achievement within the finite, combined with the sense of modes of infinitude stretching beyond each finite fact" (*MT*, 78). Nietzsche and Whitehead show great divergence on this point. Although Whitehead puts forth a doctrine of God that shows that the religious life affords the enjoyment of value in this world, he attempts to achieve more meaning for the world of Becoming with a "because."

It is not possible to eradicate this difference between Nietzsche and Whitehead, but more can be said about Whitehead's ideas of peace and the consequent nature of God in order to distinguish them from the ideas Nietzsche disdained. First, the salvific work performed by God's consequent nature is not simply a redemption that occurs wholly outside the world of Becoming. God, for Whitehead, is the supreme instance of Becoming. By maintaining that God is in, and internally related to, the world, the distinction between value achieved in the moment and the meaning it acquires *because* it remains in God's consequent nature is loosened. What is immortalized in God's consequent nature passes back into the world. "The kingdom of Heaven is with us today," Whitehead writes near the end of *Process and Reality* (*PR*, 351). The wisdom of God saves the world and this wisdom is then integrated with the primordial nature.[23] As such, the perfected wisdom of God's consequent nature finds its way back into the world and this is what Whitehead means by the claim that the kingdom of Heaven is with us today. The wisdom of God is "woven into the rhythm of mortal things" (*RM*, 155). "What is done in the world is transformed into a reality in heaven, and the reality in heaven passes back into the world. By reason of this reciprocal relation, the love in the world passes into the love in heaven, and floods back into the world" (PR 351). God's experience is not unrelated to the rest of the world. In a world constituted by actual entities that have internal relations, the experience of one actual entity is relevant to that of another. Although life, in the end, is meaningful because it matters to God, the distinction between the means and the end is not an antithetical one. "The function of being a means is not disjoined from the function of being an end. The sense of worth beyond itself is immediately enjoyed as an overpowering element in the individual self-attainment" (*PR*, 350).

Second, the feeling of peace should not be confused with Nietzsche's notion of improvement-morality or with his claim that Christianity is something of a narcotic that numbs pain. Whitehead went to great pains to avoid this connotation, worrying that his conception of peace would be confused with "the negative conception of anaesthesia" (*AI*, 285). Peace is not something we seek in exchange for a life involved in the (tragic) pursuit and creation of beauty in a finite world. "It is," rather, "a positive feeling which crowns the 'life and motion' of the soul" (*AI*, 285). The effects of peace are not a weakening of desire; peace is a tonic that "preserves the springs of energy" (*AI*, 285). Furthermore, the trust brought on by the experience of peace removes inhibitions toward pursuing a life in the world, especially a life where "the love of mankind" is present (*AI*, 286). So whereas Nietzsche stated that at the heart of the Christian life is a defensive attitude, a distrust of the strong, and a feeling of *ressentiment*, Whitehead wants to say that the experience of peace is a "barrier against narrowness" (*AI*, 286).

We must also state that peace is not a denial of tragedy. "Peace is the understanding of tragedy, and at the same time its preservation" (*AI*, 286). Peace is, I think, one of those complicated and profound feelings that Nietzsche highly valued. It is the feelings of hope and youthful trust mixed with a sense of tragedy in such a way that experience is neither superficially optimistic nor dismally pessimistic. "At the heart of the nature of things, there are always the dream of youth and the harvest of tragedy" (*AI*, 296). Peace is the "union of Youth and Tragedy" (*AI*, 296). Peace preserves tragedy by not denying that there is a tragic element to human life in the world. But it is also an understanding of tragedy in that through peace one is able to act and live in the world, trusting in the efficacy of beauty, without fearing the losses.

As an example of this point, Whitehead retells the story of the Roman general Marcus Atilius Regulus. When captured by the Carthiginarians, Regulus was sent back to Rome to deliver a series of demands that could end the war and save Regulus's life. But Regulus dissuaded Rome from accepting the terms and, on his own, went back to Carthage where he was tortured to death. "Certainly," Whitehead writes, "Regulus did not return to Carthage, with the certainty of torture and death, cherishing any mystic notions of another life— either a Christian heaven or a Buddhist Nirvana" (*AI*, 290). His courage thus was not due to the promise of a future life somewhere else but to his faith in the efficacy of his ideals and that his life had a significance that outstretched his own personal needs. "For him there was something in the world which could not be expressed as sheer personal gratification—and yet in thus sacrificing himself, his personal existence rose to its full height" (*AI*, 290). Nietzsche would have to respect Regulus, with his retention of integrity even in the face of danger and tragedy.

It should also be noted that Whitehead does not think God's consequent nature provides what has been traditionally understood as life after death in the form of "heaven" as an answer to the problem of "perpetual perishing." Whitehead left questions regarding the possibility of life after death unanswered, suggesting that the question required further evidence (see *RM*, 111). Recent Process theologians have developed different answers to the question of life after death. For example, David Griffin, combining a Whiteheadian metaphysics with empirical evidence from the field of parapsychology, argues for the possibility of a "discarnate" life after death.[24] In another vein,

Charles Hartshorne has largely followed Whitehead's neutrality on the matter, choosing instead to show that a meaningful human life does not require the prospect of subjective immortality.

Without disparaging the work of Griffin, I will follow Hartshorne's line of thinking because it better fits our present purposes and is, I think, more in line with what Whitehead himself thought.[25] Also, it is of great importance that we adhere to the claim made by both Nietzsche and Whitehead that finitude is a necessary component of meaningful experience.[26]

Hartshorne lays out two different conceptions of immortality. First, there is the traditional idea of remaining yourself after death and going on to additional experiences. Concerning this definition, Hartshorne follows what we saw Whitehead saying in chapter 6: that this sort of continuation would be an "unbearable monotony."[27] He then goes on to define a more positive meaning of immortality. Death *"is not the destruction of the reality we have achieved*. It is this reality's achievement of final definiteness, the full completion of it as gift to the world and the divine life."[28] What he means is that the finite nature of life is what gives a person's existence its final shape of definiteness. Death does not destroy past achievements but only nullifies "the not yet actualized possibilities of living."[29] Thus, in the second definition of immortality it is not the human being that is immortal, but the past achievements of the human being that go on living in God's consequent nature. We can see here that although Whitehead provides support for the idea of immortality, it is not one that denies the finite nature of human existence; neither does it trivialize the finite, as Nietzsche accused Christianity of doing. Hartshorne writes:

> I agree with the German philosopher Heidegger and his admirers, it is precisely as finite in this sense that we should love ourselves and our human fellows. . . .I need no tall stories about a supernatural kind of animal to love these persons. . . . Nor do I need such stories to love God as the all-surpassing form of love.[30]

Writing from a perspective different from Hartshorne's, Stephen Ely has argued that Whitehead's God does not satisfy the most important religious demands, especially the demand of subjective immortality. Although the fact that values are retained everlastingly in God's consequent nature, Ely argues that this fact does nothing "to alter the fact that so far as we are concerned, the evil of perishing still exists."[31] In many regards, this is true. But, in response to this demand, we might question, as did Nietzsche, the nature of the demand itself. Although tragedy can be understood, it cannot be wholly eliminated from the worldviews of Nietzsche and Whitehead. In words that Nietzsche would agree with, Hartshorne writes:

> Nothing in all this appears a sufficient reason to demand a supernatural arrangement according to which, in some unimaginable way, and in spite of the freedom without which there could be neither evil nor good, the eventual satisfaction of all wishes will be guaranteed, or at least the full rewarding and punishment of all good and bad deeds.[32]

The world, he concludes, paraphrasing Freud, "is not a kinder-garten."[33] If reality is becoming, the sort of immortality desired by Ely is simply not possible; and the desire for it is bad faith.

As I stated earlier, these comments are not intended to deny that a real difference exists between Whitehead and Nietzsche on this point about the problem of perpetual perishing. Instead, they should serve to show that not all "metaphysical comforts" are tangled up with all of the issues Nietzsche associated with Christianity.

CONCLUSION

For Whitehead, to be religious means to participate actively in the divine purpose, which is the realization of God's vision of Beauty. Such realizations are possible only within the finite world. This quest for, and realization of, beauty is a never-ending adventure. There is no final exemplification of perfect beauty. The desire for perfect, unsurpassable beauty is connected to the erroneous worldview that takes static being to be the mark of ultimate reality. If religious life is to avoid the temptation toward decadence, one must respond ever again to the lures toward new forms of beauty. "Adventure or Decadence are the only choices offered to mankind" (*AI*, 274). Eros drives God and human beings alike; we enjoy what is but wonder always, "What next?"

At the same time, this perpetual desire for novelty does not mean that the dominant mood is one of restless frustration. The achievement of intrinsic value is real, just as the enjoyment is real. Although these achievements are finite, one knows there is no other way. We, like God, should pursue Beauty with the "dream of youth," which feels no resentment, knowing full well that we will reap the "harvest of tragedy" (*AI*, 296).

Nietzsche hoped to provide the means by which one could affirm human life in the world. He readily admits (and, at times, even brags) that this is no Pollyannaish love of life but one that involves recognition of the tragic aspects of life in the world. But the tragic nature of life ought not make one timid. Rather, Nietzsche hoped for the ability to approach life with a certain relish, a certain lust. Like Whitehead's view of those involved in the adventure of the creation of beauty, Nietzsche's ideal individuals always "keep growing, keep changing." "Like trees we grow . . . not in one place only but everywhere, not in one direction but equally upward and outward and inward and downward" (*GS*, 371). They do not suffer from the desire for "rest, stillness, calm seas, redemption from themselves" (*GS*, 370). These individuals are "overfull" and have a "superabundance" of the instinct to create. These efforts involve one in tragedy, exposing them to the suffering involved in every act of creation. "All becoming and growing . . . involves pain. That there may be the eternal joy of creating, that the will to life may eternally affirm itself, the agony of the woman giving birth *must* also be there eternally" (*TI*, "What I Owe to the Ancients, 4). Along with these birth pangs there is the lucid awareness that all creations are inevitably followed by their destructions; there is the tragic knowledge that one is not redeemed from this process of creation and destruction. I imagine that Nietzsche's ideal creators also pursue beauty with "the dream of Youth," well aware of the impending "harvest of tragedy."

Indeed, Nietzsche wants us to understand that there is an insurmountable difference between Dionysus and the Crucified: "Have I been understood?—*Dionysus versus the Crucified—*" (*EH*, "Why I Am a Destiny," 9). God, he says, was "invented as a counterconcept of life—everything harmful, poisonous, slanderous, the whole hostility unto death against life synthesized in this concept in a gruesome unity!" (*EH*, "Why I Am a Destiny," 8). Indeed, it is understandable that Dionysus and certain understandings of the Crucified, God, and the religious life are ultimately irreconcilable. But, after this discussion of Whitehead's understanding of God and the religious life, we are in a position to see that it is not all that understandable that all ideas of God and the religious life are entirely antithetical to the values of Dionysus.

NOTES

1. Much of what I have to say later is greatly indebted to Donald Crosby's "Religion and Solitariness," in *Explorations in Whitehead's Philosophy*, ed. Lewis S. Ford and George L. Kline (New York: Fordham University Press, 1983), 149–69.

2. Crosby, "Religion and Solitariness," 153.

3. See David Hall, *The Civilization of Experience: A Whiteheadian Theory of Culture*, (New York: Fordham University Press, 1973), 138.

4. It would be interesting to know what Stephen Jay Gould, who was a strict orthodox Darwinian on questions concerning the purpose of evolution, would think about Whitehead's thesis. In *Full House: The Spread of Excellence from Plato to Darwin* (New York: Three Rivers Press, 1996), Gould attempts to debunk the idea that the evolutionary course has been on a narrow trajectory toward progress. The main target of his polemic is the anthropocentric idea that the purpose of evolution has been the production of human beings and that this course has been predetermined from the start. In the theory to be debased, evolution represents a ladder with single steps leading toward human beings. In contrast to this, Gould suggests that evolution should be thought of as more like a tree with many branches spreading outward, creating a world of ever greater variety and diversity. Whitehead's view that evolution entails both purpose and progress is not intended to give support to a highly anthropocentric theory.

5. John B. Cobb Jr. and David Ray Griffin, *Process Theology: An Introductory Exposition* (Philadelphia: Westminster, 1976), 43.

6. Charles Hartshorne, *Omnipotence and Other Theological Mistakes* (Albany: State University of New York Press, 1984), 10.

7. Hartshorne, *Omnipotence and Other Theological Mistakes*, 10.

8. See Griffin, *God, Power, and Evil: A Process Theodicy* (Philadelphia: Westminster, 1976), 133.

9. Johann Wolfgang von Goethe, *The Maxims and Reflections of Goethe*, trans. Bailey Saunders (New York: Macmillan and Company, 1893), 159.

10. A. H. Johnson, *Whitehead and His Philosophy* (Lanham, Md.: University Press of America, 1983), 40.

11. See David Ray Griffin, "Postmodern Theology and A/Theology," in *Varieties of Postmodern Theology* (Albany: State University of New York Press), 51.

12. Although the historical account of religion given by Whitehead is questionable and not entirely successful, it is useful, Crosby writes, "as an abstract type, which might apply in greater or lesser degree to particular religions" (Crosby, "Religion and Solitariness," 153). Furthermore, we can take "communal religion" to be a sort of foil by which Whitehead contrasts and develops his own views of what he takes to be religion to be at its best.

13. Crosby, "Religion and Solitariness," 150.

14. John B. Cobb Jr., *A Christian Natural Theology: Based on the Thought of Alfred North Whitehead* (Philadelphia: Westminster, 1965), 56.

15. Suchocki, *God, Christ, Church: A Practical Guide to Process Theology* (New York: Crossroad, 1995), 53.

16. Bernard Loomer, "S-I-Z-E Is the Measure," in *Religious Experience and Process Theology: The Pastoral Implications of a Major Movement*, ed. Harry James Cargas and Bernard Lee (New York: Paulist, 1976), 70.

17. Cobb and Griffin, *Process Theology*, 151.

18. David Griffin, "Archetypal Psychology and Process Philosophy: Complementary Postmodern Movements," in *Archetypal Process: Self and Divine in Whitehead, Jung and Hillman*, ed. David Griffin (Evanston, Ill.: Northwestern University Press, 1989), 64.

19. Griffin, "Archetypal Psychology," 65.

20. Griffin, "Archetypal Psychology," 68.

21. Cobb, *A Christian Natural Theology*, 132.

22. This thesis involves a radical departure from the classical doctrine of God. It is beyond the scope of this study to defend the claim that Whitehead's doctrine of God is in accordance with the idea of God set forth in the Christian Bible, not the demands and presuppositions of classical theology. One of Charles Hartshorne's great contributions has been to take up this task. See *The Divine Relativity: A Social Conception of God* (New Haven, Conn.: Yale University Press, 1948).

23. Randall Morris argues that because the primordial nature is an abstraction, it is fair to treat the consequent nature as "the unity of God's conceptual vision and physical feelings." See *Process Philosophy and Political Ideology: The Social and Political Thought of Alfred North Whitehead and Charles Hartshorne.* (Albany: State University of New York Press, 1991), 37.

24. See Griffin, *Parapsychology, Philosophy, and Spirituality: A Postmodern Exploration* (Albany: State University of New York Press, 1997), 96–168.

25. This is not to say that Griffin's argument deviates from Whitehead's philosophy. Rather, it follows a line of thought that Whitehead did not follow. Furthermore, I do not think that Griffin's suggestions make him liable to a line of criticism from Nietzsche's perspective. About his idea of life after death, Griffin writes, "It would not necessarily mean returning to traditional views of heaven and hell. It would also not necessarily mean returning to a form of spirituality in which the importance of the present life is understood primarily as a preparation for a future life" (*Religion and Scientific Naturalism,* 240).

26. Interestingly, Griffin seems to amend his own view of life after death with the recognition that meaningfulness does not require that an individual human life be everlasting. "What we know, at most, is only that people, at least most people, want more life. We do not know that after having more

life for a considerable period—perhaps ten thousand, a hundred thousand, an million, or a billion years—we would want to continue having new experiences." (*Reenchantment without Supernaturalism: Postmodern Proposals* [Albany: State University of New York Press, 1988], 240).

27. Hartshorne, *Omnipotence and Other Theological Mistakes*, 35.

28. Hartshorne, *Omnipotence and Other Theological Mistakes*, 35.

29. Hartshorne, *Omnipotence and Other Theological Mistakes*, 36

30. Hartshorne, *Omnipotence and Other Theological Mistakes*, 36.

31. Stephen Ely, "The Religious Availability of Whitehead's God: A Critical Analysis," in *Explorations in Whitehead's Philosophy*, 200.

32. Hartshorne, *Omnipotence and Other Theological* Mistakes, 37.

33. Hartshorne, *Omnipotence and Other Theological* Mistakes, 37.

9

Conclusion

> Those who would take over the earth
> And shape it to their will
> Never, I notice, succeed
>
> —*Lao Tzu*, The Way of Life

In the preceding pages, we have seen that one of the fundamental differences between Nietzsche and Whitehead is whether the meaning of human life is connected to some greater cosmic purpose. For Nietzsche, the death of God is both an undeniable event and a welcomed one. Without God, human beings are liberated from a nihilistic system of values and are now free to create their own meanings and values. For Whitehead, while the death of the supernatural God is a welcomed event, the loss of all ideas of God grounding a cosmic purpose altogether has disastrous consequences. Those consequences require that we seek alternative conceptions of these ideas. Although it is possible to criticize Whitehead's solution to the problem of nihilism on the basis of Nietzsche's criteria for a thoroughly "this-worldly" solution, I would like to conclude this study with some reasons why I think Nietzsche's atheistic philosophy comes up short and how Whitehead's theistic cosmology avoids these shortcomings.

As we saw, the death of God, for Nietzsche, shows reality to be a vast and open sea that provides us with the opportunity to live lives in which we are free to create our own values. The lion's slaughter of the great dragon named "Thou Shalt" means that one is liberated from the idea that values are inscribed within the fabric of reality. All values are human creations. This point includes not only ethical and religious values, but the values we give to the natural world. "Nature is always value-less" (*GS*, 301). As Joan Stambaugh writes, "There is no 'reality' already 'there' waiting for us."[1] Therefore, "finding" the meaning of life requires that we give up the idea that it is something to be discovered; rather, the meaning of human life in the world is to be created. To be sure, saying that there is no "reality" there waiting for us does not mean there is no reality. It means only that reality is chaos, that it does not come to us with some pre-inscribed value. "The total character of the world, however, is in all eternity chaos— in the sense not of a lack of necessity but of a lack of order, arrangement, form, beauty, wisdom, and whatever other names there are for our aesthetic anthropomorphisms" (*GS*, 109). Our values of beauty and morality simply do not apply to the world. The world is "neither perfect, nor beautiful, nor noble, nor does it wish to become any of these things" (*GS*, 109). All values are interpretations. Chaos is the only reality.

Nietzsche thinks that this situation has great potential. The death of God and the revelation that reality is a chaotic Becoming, unrelieved by any grand ahistorical end, presents a host of liberating possibilities. Although this open and valueless sea provides a way for human beings to construe their individual lives as meaningful through self-creation, it does not, I contend, show that human life *in the world* is or even can be meaningful. By this, I mean that while Nietzsche's philosophy provides a poignant expression of how we can find the world to be a *space* in which we can create ourselves, it does not present the world to be a *place* where we encounter other intrinsically valuable entities. An intrinsically valuable entity is an entity that is something for itself. If reality is valueless and all values are self-creations, then that with which I interact—be it other people or anything else that presents itself to experience—does not contribute anything significant to experience except an opportunity for me to make something out of it. If another does not contribute something positive to experience, then my experience with that entity is meaningless in the sense that the experienced entity is not constitutive of my experience.

One way of understanding what I am saying is to draw an analogy to Kierkegaards's criticism of Socrates in *Philosophical Fragments*. The book opens with an exposition of how Socrates answers the question of whether the Truth can be learned. Socrates states that a person cannot seek what he or she does not already know. Learning cannot be construed as a process in which the student comes into something new. For Socrates, learning is to be thought of as a process of *recollection*. Everything there is to know is already within the individual. The individual is not in a state of lack. Rather, the problem of existence is merely a problem of ignorance, of having this knowledge clouded over. Therefore, teachers only deliver students to themselves. The teacher is a "midwife." Nothing new, nothing previously unknown to the student, is brought by the teacher.

What Kierkegaard criticizes is the fact that this view makes the individual identity of the teacher unimportant.[2] Teachers can be replaced and interchanged with no necessary difference in result. Furthermore, if everything is always already known within the individual, the moment in time in which the remembrance occurs is meaningless. Neither people nor moments in time bring something new. Kierkegaard captures both of these points in the following passage:

> If I were to imagine myself meeting Socrates, Prodicus, or the maidservant in another life, there again none of them would be more than an occasion, as Socrates intrepidly expresses it by saying that even in the underworld he would only ask questions, for the ultimate idea in all questioning is that the person asked must himself possess the truth and acquire it by himself. The temporal point of departure is nothing, because in the same moment I discover that I have known the truth from eternity without knowing it, then the same instant that moment is hidden in the eternal, assimilated into it in such a way that I, so to speak, still cannot find it even if I were to look for it, because there is no Here and no There, but only an *ubique et nusquam*.[3]

The analogy I want to draw is that Nietzsche's view is, in this case, similar to that of Socrates. By stating that the meaning and value of any experience are solely the product of the value creator, Nietzsche makes the world meaningless for our existence in the same way that Socrates, as construed by Kierkegaard, makes the individual identity of the teacher meaningless. Because all meaning is self-created, we cannot state that our relationships with others contribute something unavailable anywhere else. They provide only an opportunity, only a road to ourselves. While, for Nietzsche, we may flow into the world, the world does not flow into us.

An aspect of Heidegger's criticism of Nietzsche speaks to my point. With Nietzsche's call that we become value creators, says Heidegger, the world becomes nothing more than an object. "The world changes into object. In this revolutionary objectifying of everything that is, the earth, that which first of all must be put at the disposal of representing and setting forth, moves into the midst of human positing and analyzing."[4] Treated only as the medium for the insertion of value, "the earth itself can show itself only as the object of assault, an assault that, in human willing, establishes itself as unconditional objectification."[5] For this reason, Heidegger takes Nietzsche to be the culmination of the Western metaphysical tradition and still a part of its nihilistic trajectory. Like Socrates, Christianity, modern philosophy, science, and technology, Nietzsche's philosophy continues the struggle for the domination of the earth. By doing so, Nietzsche, according to Heidegger, continues the forgetfulness of Being. "If, however, value does not let Being be Being, does not let it be what it is as Being itself, then this supposed overcoming is above all the consummation of nihilism."[6]

What I take Heidegger's central point to be is that Nietzsche's proposal cuts off any possibility for one to listen to Being. Unlike the pre-Socratics who fulfilled their existence by opening and exposing themselves to "what is,"[7] Nietzsche is reluctant to listen because he thinks there is nothing to hear. The world is available for our use. We put value into the world but derive none from it.

Although it would seem that Nietzsche's criticism of the various strands of latent nihilism as practices that presuppose a hostility between a human being and the world would lead him toward a solution that avoids such a hostility, his solution to overcoming the nihilism that follows the death of God retains that hostility. The relationship between the value creator and the objects on which we create is not one of reciprocity. The ascetic priest criticized by Nietzsche is hostile toward the world insofar as he treats it only as a bridge to a greater reality (*GM*, III:11). But in this case, so does Nietzsche. "Life is *essentially* appropriation, injury, overpowering of what is alien and weaker. . . . But why should one always use those words in which a slanderous intent has been imprinted for ages?" (*BGE*, 259). Nietzsche's attempt to take the slander out of this sort of life amounts to his defense of the will to power and the artistic, creative life.[8]

In his comparison of Nietzsche's "will to power" and the Chinese understanding of "virtuality" (*de*), Roger Ames concludes with the following contrast:

> Unlike virtuality (*de*), the emphasis [in the will to power] is not upon the mutuality and interdependence of these centers, where they enhance and become coextensive with one another by accommodating direction and impulse. Instead, the language is often of one center "consuming" another to express it in its own valuations.[9]

Nietzsche's understanding of the will to power and the possibility of a transvaluation of values, Ames continues, requires a feeling of antagonism. Nietzsche's proposal can succeed, Ames states, in generating a feeling of joy. But this feeling of joy, he continues, is not "enjoyment."[10] Enjoyment requires a sense of sharing and mutuality. It requires that one be open to the influence of others.[11]

To be sure, there are some passages in which Nietzsche does seem to be suggesting that life in the world is meaningful in a way that it has something more to offer than being merely a blank space. For example, in *The Gay Science*, Nietzsche states that what distinguishes "higher" human beings from the "lower" is "that the former see and hear immeasurably more, and see and hear thoughtfully" (*GS*, 301). But in this example, he backs off from the full import of this suggestion by reminding the reader that these feelings are themselves self-created fictions. Although the "higher" human being may see and hear "immeasurably" more, "he can never shake off a *delusion*" (*GS*, 301). The delusion exists because what is seen and heard is self-created. Being in the world is a process of eisegesis, not exegesis. Although Nietzsche directs much of his attention to the development of a philosophy that purports an affirmation of human existence in spite of the death of God, he is unable to show that life *in the world* is meaningful *because* of the structure of reality.

In Whitehead's "live" universe, constituted by actual entities that are accomplishments of value, experience is meaningful *within* the world and *because* of the world. In the first phase of experience, experience in the mode of causal efficacy, we feel the "pressure from a world of things with characters in their own right, characters mysteriously moulding our own natures" (*S*, 44). What Whitehead so greatly appreciated about the poetry of Wordsworth and Shelley was that they connected their experience of beauty with something going on in the world. The experience of beauty is not wholly the production of human subjectivity. When I experience something as beautiful, it is largely a result of the fact that the experienced entity *is* beautiful. For example, when you hate or love, there is an entity that you are either retreating from or expanding toward. "You cannot retreat from mere subjectivity" (*S*, 45). The past world presents its accomplishments to the concrescing actual entity. We react to these achieved values. These accomplishments are constitutive of the present. We are internally related to the past, and, in contrast to Nietzsche's sometimes expressed opinion, the quality of experience depends on these relations.

The main difference between Whitehead and Nietzsche on this point is that for Whitehead the world flows into the person and the person flows back into the world. For Nietzsche, it is only the person that flows into the world. At times Zarathustra senses these problems and laments that he can only be a gift giver and not a receiver of the gifts of others. "I do not know the happiness of those who receive" (*Z*, II:9). As a giver who cannot enjoy the gifts of others, Zarathustra often experiences the dark night of loneliness: "Oh, the loneliness of all givers! Oh, the taciturnity of all who shine!" (*Z*, II:9). Those who can only give have no one to talk to, no one to listen to. They are reluctant to join in the conversation. In the end, Nietzsche's presents us with a lonely enterprise. This loneliness is expressed in Nietzsche's description of the "free spirit":

> One lives without being any longer in the fetters of love and hate, without Yes, without No, near or far off by one's will, preferably slipping away, evading, fluttering off, flying once again upward and away; one is spoiled like anyone who has ever seen a tremendous abundance of things *beneath* him—and one becomes the opposite of those who concern themselves with things that have nothing to do with them. (*HATH*, preface, 4)[12]

The second problem with Nietzsche's atheistic affirmation of life is that if reality is forever valueless and chaotic, it is difficult to see how the values we create to give our lives meaning can have any gravity or power to sustain us. How can our newly created values be believed to be true when the death of God makes any claim to truth impossible? One must believe that, in one way or another, the values and meanings we give to existence have some sort of truth or efficacy. Nietzsche admits this in his notebooks. "There is one great paralysis:

to work *in vain*, to struggle in vain" (*WP*, 597; 1886–1887). The problem here, as Stanley Rosen writes, is that the creative stage "is already vitiated by the destructive force of the first substage."[13] If the death of God and the destructive work of the lion reveal the nature of reality, how can creative activity create anything more than a delusion? To believe in the self-created ideals we live by is to believe in a lie. It is impossible, Rosen writes, "to pull a rabbit out of an empty hat."[14] Any meaning given to existence is sure to evaporate as the creators come to see their own hands in the process. Will not the process of creation in this world eventually meet with indifference? Is it not likely that we will find ourselves in a situation similar to the one experienced by Hegel's master when he realizes that the slave's recognition of him is not authentic?[15]

It seems that the project of creating new values in a world forever chaotic can only give life a new sense of meaningfulness if the creator somehow forgets that these new values are simply self-created. Consider Nietzsche's attempt to overcome nihilism through tragic art. According to Nietzsche, the wisdom of Silenus—which states that in a Dionysian world of Becoming, it is best not to have been born at all, thus saving a human being from a life of suffering—can be reversed through tragic art. In tragic art, the hero faces the Dionysian core of reality with a sense of dignity, strength, and integrity. In tragedy, the horrible is transformed into the sublime. The tragic figure nobly meets his or her fate in this world and does not basely suffer from it.[16] The tragic figure lives on the ideal that it is better to face the Dionysian core of reality courageously rather than sheepishly. In this way, tragedy presents us with possibilities that can, as Schacht writes, "carry us beyond the mere acknowledgment of intractable aspects of the human condition, enabling us to discern ways in which the latter may be confronted and transformed into occasions for the endowment of life with grandeur and dignity."[17] The problem is that these images do not, as Schacht admits, "confront us with the truth of human existence."[18] They are illusions in that tragedy "no less than beauty may be said to exist only in the eye of the beholder, whose sensibility has been formed and cultivated by art."[19] The tragic figure sustains his or her existence by means of an ideal that does not correspond to the ways of reality. But if one is trying to live with a degree of intellectual integrity, as Nietzsche insists we do, this ideal can have no power.

As we have seen, Nietzsche does attempt to correct this problem in his later writings by means of the notion that Becoming is innocent. But his correctives cannot get beyond the necessity of forgetting that reality is valueless. For Nietzsche, one of the great charms of the child is its ability to live without any concerns as to whether the child's creations are true or false. But one of the things that occurs in the transformation from the lion to the child is a "forgetting" (*Z*, I:1). Nietzsche does not say exactly what is forgotten, but a case can be made for suggesting that what is forgotten is what the lion has revealed: the fundamental value-lessness of nature. The child does not participate in the world as it truly is. In some respects, the child is the one who has learned the lesson of Nietzsche's essay *The Utility and Liability of History.*

> In the case of the smallest and the greatest happiness, it is always just one thing alone that makes happiness happiness: the ability to forget, or, expressed in a more scholarly fashion, the capacity to feel ahistorically over the entire course of its duration. (*ULH*, 1)

Forgetting is necessary because the one "who is damned to see becoming everywhere . . . would no longer believe in his own being . . . would see everything flow apart in turbulent particles" (*ULH*, 1).

One could argue that Nietzsche's doctrine of eternal return serves to overcome this problem. As an existential imperative, it attributes almost a maddening amount of significance to everything we do. We are to live, make choices, and pursue goals *as if* we were destined to live our lives again and again. But when understood as only an existential imperative, the doctrine of eternal return falls back into the problem of making life meaningful in a valueless cosmos by means of an illusion. We are still not living in reality on reality's terms. Notice that the doctrine is called "eternal return of the same," not "live once, only once, and never more." We are not living as if every moment, every creative achievement, were subject to dissipation. Rather, we are living as if we must live our lives again, which gives rise to the suspicion that Nietzsche is resorting, despite his probable protest against Whitehead's concept of God's consequent nature, to some form of redemption from transience. In his notebooks, Nietzsche writes:

> A certain emperor always bore in mind the transitoriness of all things so as not to take them too seriously and to live at peace among them. To me, on the contrary, everything seems far too valuable to be so fleeting: I seek an eternity for everything. . . . *My consolation is that everything that has been is eternal* (*WP*, 1065; 1887–1888; emphasis added).

After quoting this just-cited passage, David Krell writes:

> Here the idea of eternal recurrence as a test, as the most difficult and most burdensome thought, as the tragic thought that would separate overman from the all-too-human, dwindles to a paltry consolation, to the decadence of redemption. How close the communication of Dionysian affirmation brings us to the Redeemer type.[20]

Although Whitehead agrees that reality is Becoming and that "perpetual perishing" is an ontological fact, his answer to these facts avoids these problems. The presence of God in the universe allows Whitehead to say that the ideals we live by are ontologically grounded. Whereas Nietzsche must say that the courage and nobility of the tragic hero is an illusion, Whitehead can say that a courageous and noble individual is living in accordance with one of God's aims for the world. This fact gives ideals the weight and importance they need if they are effectively to sustain us. In addition, Whitehead's thought can provide us with a way of understanding the important aspects of Nietzsche's doctrine of the eternal return as an existential imperative. We ought to act, make choices, and pursue goals that we could live with everlastingly because they do actually live everlastingly in God's consequent nature. Even in a world wrought by perpetual perishing, sheer and meaningless transience is not the whole story. "Pereunt et imputantur," Whitehead says.

> Here "Pereunt" refers to the world disclosed in the immediate presentation, gay with a thousand tints, passing, and intrinsically meaningless. "Imputantur" refers to the world disclosed in its causal efficacy, where each event infects the ages to come, for good or evil, with its own individuality. (*S*, 47)

Not only does Whitehead's doctrine of God avoid Nietzsche's connection between God and the denigration of human life in the world, but also it provides answers to problems that undermine Nietzsche's own proposal for the affirmation of human existence in the world.

NOTES

1. Joan Stambaugh, *The Other Nietzsche* (Albany: State University of New York Press, 1994), 123.

2. Of course, Kierkergaard is interested in establishing the unique identity of Jesus Christ and the identity between message and messenger that occurs in his person.

3. Søren Kierkegaard, *Philosophical Fragments*, trans. Howard V. Hong and Edna H. Hong (Princeton, N.J.: Princeton University Press, 1985), 12–13.

4. Martin Heidegger, "The Word of Nietzsche: 'God is Dead,'" in *The Question Concerning Technology and Other Essays*, trans. William Lovitt (New York: Harper Torchbooks, 1977), 100.

5. Heidegger, "The Word of Nietzsche," 100.

6. Heidegger, "The Word of Nietzsche," 104.

7. Heidegger, "The Age of the World Picture," in *The Question Concerning Technology and Other Essays*, trans. William Lovitt (New York: Harper Torchbooks, 1977), 131.

8. I think that the effort of Max Hallman in "Nietzsche's Environmental Ethics," *Environmental Ethics* 13 (1991): 99, to show that Nietzsche's philosophy "is compatible with an ecologically oriented, environmentally concerned philosophizing" is mistaken. He argues that Nietzsche's idea that reality is "will to power" contains a vision of the world as a "living, growing, decaying process, a process in which everything that exists is intertwined in a dynamic play of creation and recreation" (123). Although this is true, the thesis provides no reason why one ought to be environmentally sensitive to nature. If nature is valueless, what would be the harm in destroying it?

9. Roger Ames, "Nietzsche's 'Will to Power' and Chinese 'Virtuality' (*De*): A Comparative Study," in *Nietzsche and Asian Thought*, ed. Graham Parkes (Chicago: University of Chicago Press, 1991), 147.

10. Ames, "Nietzsche's 'Will to Power, and Chinese Virtuality (*De*)," 148.

11. When giving a sort of typology of personalities in *I and Thou*, Martin Buber admits that Napoleon was a great individual, singly determined by a great sense of purpose. Everything in the world, everything that he comes across "becomes It and subservient to his cause." See *I and Thou*, trans. Walter Kaufmann (New York: Scribners, 1970), 117. Because Napoleon sees the world only in terms of his cause, Buber writes that he "participates in no actuality, but others participate immeasurably in him as in an actuality" (118). In the end, Napoleon lacks the power to relate and, as a result, his "I-saying is not vitally emphatic, not full" (118). Napoleon has many characteristics similar to Zarathustra. Nietzsche is a great fan of Napoleon, citing him as one of his "good Europeans" (*BGE*, 256).

12. Although *Human, All Too Human* was written in 1878, this preface was written in 1886, making it contemporary with *Zarathustra*.

13. Stanley Rosen, *The Mask of Enlightenment: Nietzsche's Zarathustra* (Cambridge: Cambridge University Press, 1995), 6.

14. Rosen, *The Mask of Enlightenment*, 249.

15. See *Phenomenology of Spirit*, trans. A. V. Miller (Oxford: Oxford University Press, 1977), 117.

16. Richard Schacht, *Making Sense of Nietzsche: Reflections Timely and Untimely* (Urbana: University of Illinois Press, 1995), 148.

17. Schacht, *Making Sense of Nietzsche*, 149.

18. Schacht, *Making Sense of Nietzsche*, 149.

19. Schacht, *Making Sense of Nietzsche*, 151.

20. David Farrell Krell, *Infectious Nietzsche* (Bloomington: Indiana University Press, 1996), 77.

Bibliography

Abrams, M. H. *Natural Supernaturalism: Tradition and Revolution in Romantic Literature*. New York: Norton, 1971.

Babich, Babette E. *Nietzsche's Philosophy of Science: Reflecting Science on the Ground of Art and Life*. Albany: State University of New York Press, 1994.

Berkowitz, Peter. *Nietzsche: The Ethics of an Immoralist*. Cambridge, Mass.: Harvard University Press, 1995.

Bishop, Elizabeth. "One Art," in *The Complete Poems 1927–1979*. New York: Farrar, Straus & Giroux.

Bloom, Alan. *The Closing of the American Mind*. New York: Simon & Schuster, 1987.

Brooke, John Hedley. *Science and Religion: Some Historical Perspectives*. Cambridge: Cambridge University Press, 1991.

Buber, Martin. *I and Thou*. Translated by Walter Kaufmann. New York: Scribner's, 1970.

Burgard, Peter, ed. *Nietzsche and the Feminine*. Charlottesville: University of Virginia Press, 1994.

Carr, Karen L. *The Banalization of Nihilism: Twentieth Century Responses to Meaninglessness*. Albany: State University of New York Press, 1992.

Christian, William A. *An Interpretation of Whitehead's Metaphysics*. New Haven, Conn.: Yale University Press, 1959.

Cobb, John B., Jr. *A Christian Natural Theology: Based on the Thought of Alfred North Whitehead*. Philadelphia: Westminster, 1965.

———. *God and World*. Philadelphia: Westminster, 1969.

———. "Response to Reynolds." In *John Cobb's Theology in Process*. Edited by David Ray Griffin and Thomas J. J. Altizer. Philadelphia: Westminster, 1977, 181–82.

Cobb, John B., Jr., and David Ray Griffin. *Process Theology: An Introductory Exposition*. Philadelphia: Westminster, 1976.

Cronin, Helena. *The Ant and the Peacock: Altruism and Sexual Selection from Darwin to Today*. Cambridge: Cambridge University Press, 1991.

Dannhauser, Werner J. *Nietzsche's View of Socrates*. Ithaca, N.Y.: Cornell University Press, 1974.

Deleuze, Gilles. *Nietzsche and Philosophy*. Translated by Hugh Tomlinson. New York: Columbia University Press, 1962.

Donnelley, Strachan. "Whitehead and Nietzsche: Overcoming the Evil of Time." *Process Studies* 12, no. 1 (Spring, 1982): 1–14.

Ferré, Frederick. *Being and Value: Toward a Constructive Postmodern Metaphysics*. Albany: State University of New York Press, 1996.

Ferrucci, Franco. *The Life of God (as Told by Himself)*. Translated by Raymond Rosenthal and Franco Ferrucci. Chicago: University of Chicago Press, 1996.

Gare, Arran. *Beyond European Civilization: Marxism, Process Philosophy and the Environment*. Bungendore, Australia: Eco-Logical, 1993.

———. *Nihilism Incorporated: European Civilization and Environmental Destruction*. Bungendore, Australia: Eco-Logical, 1993.

Gillespie, Michael Allen. *Nihilism before Nietzsche*. Chicago: University of Chicago Press, 1995.

Goethe, Johann Wolfgang von. *The Maxims and Reflections of Goethe*. Translated and edited by Bailey Saunders. New York: Macmillan, 1893.

Gould, Stephen Jay. *Full House: The Spread of Excellence from Plato to Darwin*. New York: Three Rivers, 1996.

Greene, John. *Science, Ideology, and World View: Essays in the History of Evolutionary Ideas*. Berkeley: University of California Press, 1981.

Griffin, David Ray. *God and Religion in the Postmodern World: Essays in Postmodern Theology*. Albany: State University of New York Press, 1989.

———. *God, Power, and Evil: A Process Theodicy*. Philadelphia: Westminster, 1976.

———. *Parapsychology, Philosophy, and Spirituality: A Postmodern Exploration*. Albany: State University of New York Press, 1997

———. *Religion and Scientific Naturalism: Overcoming the Conflicts*. Albany: State University of New York Press, 2000.

———. *Unsnarling the World-Knot: Consciousness, Freedom, and the Mind-Body Problem*. Berkeley: University of California Press, 1998.

———, ed. *Archetypal Process: Self and Divine in Whitehead, Jung and Hillman*. Evanston, Ill.: Northwestern University Press, 1989.

———, ed. *The Reenchantment of Science: Postmodern Proposals*. Albany: State University of New York Press, 1988.

———, ed. *Varieties of Postmodern Theology*. Albany: State University of New York Press.

Griffin, David Ray, et al. *Founders of Constructive Postmodern Philosophy: Peirce, James, Bergson, Whitehead, and Hartshorne*. Albany: State University of New York Press, 1993.

Haar Michel. *Nietzsche and Metaphysics*. Translated and edited by Michael Gendre. Albany: State University of New York Press, 1996.

Hall, David L. *The Civilization of Experience: A Whiteheadian Theory of Culture*. New York: Fordham University Press, 1973.

———. *Eros and Irony: A Prelude to Philosophical Anarchism*. Albany: State University of New York Press, 1982.

Hallman, Max. "Nietzsche's Environmental Ethics." *Environmental Ethics* 13 (1991).

Harpham, Geoffrey Galt. *The Ascetic Imperative in Culture and Criticism*. Chicago: University of Chicago Press, 1987.

Hartshorne, Charles. *The Divine Relativity: A Social Conception of God*. New Haven, Conn.: Yale University Press, 1948.

———. *Omnipotence and Other Theological Mistakes*. Albany: State University of New York Press, 1984.

Harsthorne, Charles, and William Reese. *Philosophers Speak of God*. New York: Humanity, 2000.

Harvey, David. *The Condition of Postmodernity*. Oxford: Blackwell, 1990.

Hegel, G. W. F. *Phenomenology of Spirit*. Translated by A. V. Miller. Oxford: Oxford University Press, 1977.

Heidegger, Martin. *Nietzsche*. 4 vols. Translated and edited by David Farrell Krell. San Francisco: Harper San Francisco, 1991.

———. *The Question Concerning Technology and Other Essays*. Translated by William Lovitt. New York: Harper & Row, 1977.

Higgins, Kathleen Marie. *Nietzsche's Zarathustra*. Philadelphia: Temple University Press, 1987.

Hollingdale, R. J. *Nietzsche: The Man and His Philosophy*. London: Routledge & Kegan Paul, 1965.

Hosinski, Thomas E. *Stubborn Fact and Creative Advance: An Introduction to the Metaphysics of Alfred North Whitehead*. Lanham, Md.: Rowman & Littlefield, 1993.

Hume, David. *A Treatise of Human Nature*. Edited by L. A. Selby-Bigge. Oxford: Clarendon, 1951.

Ingraffia, Brian. *Postmodern Theory and Biblical Theology*. Cambridge: Cambridge University Press, 1995.

Johnson, A. H. *Whitehead and His Philosophy*. Lanham, Md.: University Press of America, 1983.

Jones, W. T. *History of Western Philosophy*. Vol. 5, *The Twentieth Century to Wittgenstein and Sartre*. New York: Harcourt Brace Jovanovich, 1975.

Kaufmann, Walter. *Nietzsche: Philosopher, Psychologist, Antichrist*, 4th ed. Princeton, N.J.: Princeton University Press, 1974.

Kline, George L., ed. *Alfred North Whitehead: Essays on His Philosophy*. Englewood Cliffs, N. J.: Prentice Hall, 1963.

Kofman, Sarah. *Nietzsche and Metaphor*. Translated by Duncan Large. Stanford, Calif.: Stanford University Press, 1993.

———. "Nietzsche's Socrates: 'Who Is Socrates?'" *Graduate Faculty Journal* 15, no 2 (1991): 7–30.

Krell, David Farrell. *Infectious Nietzsche*. Bloomington: Indiana University Press, 1996.

———, ed. *Exceedingly Nietzsche*. London: Routledge, 1988.

Kundera, Milan. *The Unbearable Lightness of Being*. Translated by Michael Henry Heim. New York: Harper & Row, 1984.

Lampert, Laurence. *Nietzsche and Modern Times: A Study of Bacon, Descartes, and Nietzsche*. New Haven, Conn.: Yale University Press, 1993.

Lasch, Christopher. *The Culture of Narcissism: American Life in an Age of Diminishing Expectations*. New York: Norton, 1979.

Leclerc, Ivor. *Whitehead's Metaphysics: An Introductory Exposition*. Bloomington: Indiana University Press, 1975.

Levin, David Michael, ed. *Modernity and the Hegemony of Vision*. Berkeley: University of California Press, 1993.

———. *Pathologies of the Modern Self: Postmodern Studies on Narcissism, Schizophrenia, and Depression*. New York: New York University Press, 1987.

Loomer, Bernard. "S-I-Z-E Is the Measure." In *Religious Experience and Process Theology: The Pastoral Implications of a Major Movement*, ed. Harry James Cargas and Bernard Lee. New York: Paulist, 1976.

Lowe, Victor. *Alfred North Whitehead: The Man and His Work*. Vol. 1, *1861–1910*. Baltimore: Johns Hopkins University Press, 1985.

———. *Alfred North Whitehead: The Man and His Work*. Vol. 2, *1910–1947*. Edited by J. B. Schneewind. Baltimore: Johns Hopkins University Press, 1990.

Löwith, Karl. *From Hegel to Nietzsche: The Revolution in Nineteenth-Century Thought*. Translated by David E. Green. New York: Columbia University Press, 1964.

———. *Nietzsche's Philosophy of the Eternal Recurrence of the Same*. Translated by J. Harvey Lomax. Berkeley: University of California Press, 1997.

Lucas, George R. Jr. *The Rehabilitation of Whitehead: An Analytic and Historical Assessment of Process Philosophy*. Albany: State University of New York Press, 1989.

Magnus, Bernd. *Nietzsche's Existential Imperative*. Bloomington: Indiana University Press, 1978.

Morgan, George A. *What Nietzsche Means*. Cambridge, Mass.: Harvard University Press, 1941; Harper Torchbooks, 1965.

Morris, Randall C. *Process Philosophy and Political Ideology: The Social and Political Thought of Alfred North Whitehead and Charles Hartshorne*. Albany: State University of New York Press, 1991.

Nehamas, Alexander. *Nietzsche: Life as Literature*. Cambridge, Mass.: Harvard University Press, 1985.

Nietzsche, Friedrich. *The Antichrist*. In *The Portable Nietzsche*. Translated and edited by Walter Kaufmann. New York: Penguin, 1982, 565–656.

———. *Beyond Good and Evil: Prelude to a Philosophy of the Future*. Translated by Walter Kaufmann. New York: Vintage, 1966.

———. *The Birth of Tragedy*. In *The Birth of Tragedy and The Case of Wagner*. Translated by Walter Kaufmann. New York: Vintage, 1967.

———. *The Case of Wagner*. In *The Birth of Tragedy and The Case of Wagner*. Translated by Walter Kaufmann. New York: Vintage, 1967.

———. *Daybreak: Thoughts on the Prejudices of Morality*. Translated by R. J. Hollingdale. Cambridge: Cambridge University Press, 1982.

———. *Ecce Homo: Or How One Becomes What One Is*. In *On the Genealogy of Morals and Ecce Homo*. Translated by Walter Kaufmann. New York: Vintage, 1974.

———. *The Gay Science*. Translated by Walter Kaufmann. New York: Vintage, 1974.

———. *Human, All Too Human, I: A Book for Free Spirits*. Translated by Gary Handwerk. Stanford, Calif.: Stanford University Press, 1995.

———. *On the Genealogy of Morals*. In *On the Genealogy of Morals and Ecce Homo*. Translated by Walter Kaufmann. New York: Vintage, 1989.

———. *On Truth and Lie in an Extra-Moral Sense*. In *The Portable Nietzsche*. Translated and edited by Walter Kaufmann. New York: Penguin, 1982, 42–47.

———. *Selected Letters of Friedrich Nietzsche*. Translated and edited by Christopher Middleton. Chicago: University of Chicago Press, 1969.

———. *Thus Spoke Zarathustra*. In *The Portable Nietzsche*. Translated and edited by Walter Kaufmann. New York: Penguin, 1982, 103–439.

———. *Twilight of the Idols*. In *The Portable Nietzsche*. Translated and edited by Walter Kaufmann. New York: Penguin, 1982, 463–563.

———. *Unfashionable Observations*. Translated by Richard T. Gray. Stanford, Calif.: Stanford University Press, 1995.

———. *The Will to Power*. Translated by Walter Kaufmann and R. J. Holingdale. New York: Vintage, 1968.

Nussbaum, Martha. *The Fragility of Goodness: Luck and Ethics in Greek Tragedy and Philosophy*. Cambridge: Cambridge University Press, 1986.

Parkes, Graham, ed. *Nietzsche and Asian Thought*. Chicago: University of Chicago Press, 1991.

Pelikan, Jaroslav. *The Christian Tradition: A History of the Development of Doctrine*. Vol. I, *The Emergence of the Catholic Tradition (100–600)*. Chicago: University of Chicago Press, 1971.

Plato. *The Collected Dialogues*. Edited by Edith Hamilton and Huntington Cairns. Princeton, N.J.: Princeton University Press, 1961.

Riedel, Manfred. "The 'Wondrous Double Nature' of Philosophy: Nietzsche's Determination of Thinking among the Greeks." *Graduate Faculty Philosophy Journal* (New School for Social Research) 15, no. 2 (1991): 49–66.

Roberts, Tyler. *Contesting Spirit: Nietzsche, Affirmation, Religion.* Princeton, N.J.: Princeton University Press, 1998.

Rosen, Stanley. *The Mask of Enlightenment: Nietzsche's Zarathustra.* Cambridge: Cambridge University Press, 1995.

Said, Edward W. *Orientalism.* New York: Vintage, 1979.

Sallis, John. *Nietzsche and the Space of Tragedy.* Chicago: University of Chicago Press, 1991.

Schacht, Richard. *Making Sense of Nietzsche: Reflections Timely and Untimely.* Urbana: University of Illinois Press, 1995.

———. *Nietzsche.* London: Routledge, 1983.

Schilpp, Paul Arthur, ed. *The Philosophy of Alfred North Whitehead.* LaSalle, Ill.: Open Court, 1951.

Schopenhauer, Arthur. *The World as Will and Idea.* Vol. 1. Translated by R. B. Haldane and J. Kemp. London: Routledge & Kegan Paul, 1957.

Schrift, Alan D. *Nietzsche and the Question of Interpretation: Between Hermeneutics and Deconstruction.* New York: Routledge, 1990.

Shakespeare, William. *Hamlet.* Edited by David Bevington. New York: Bantam, 1988.

Shapiro, Gary. *Nietzschean Narratives.* Bloomington: Indiana University Press, 1989.

Silk, M. S., and J. P. Stern. *Nietzsche on Tragedy.* Cambridge: Cambridge University Press, 1981.

Smith, Gregory Bruce. *Nietzsche, Heidegger and the Transition to Postmodernity.* Chicago: University of Chicago Press, 1996.

Stambaugh, Joan. *The Other Nietzsche.* Albany: State University of New York Press, 1994.

Stevens, Wallace. *The Collected Poems.* New York: Vintage, 1990.

Suchocki, Marjorie. *The End of Evil: Process Eschatology in Historical Context.* Albany: State University of New York Press, 1988.

———. *God, Christ, Church: A Practical Guide to Process Theology.* New York: Crossroad, 1995.

Thatcher, David S. *Nietzsche in England 1890–1914.* Toronto: University of Toronto Press, 1970.

Thiele, Leslie. *Friedrich Nietzsche and the Politics of the Soul: A Study of Heroic Individualism.* Princeton, N.J.: Princeton University Press, 1990.

Wesson, Robert. *Beyond Natural Selection.* Cambridge, Mass.: MIT Press, 1991.

White, Alan. "Nietzschean Nihilism: A Typology." *International Studies in Philosophy* 19 (Summer, 1987): 29–44.

White, Hayden. *Metahistory: The Historical Imagination in Nineteenth-Century Europe.* Baltimore: Johns Hopkins University Press, 1973.

Whitehead, Alfred North. *Adventures of Ideas*. New York: Free Press, 1933.
———. *The Function of Reason*. Boston: Beacon, 1929.
———. "Immortality." In *Science and Philosophy*. New York: Philosophical Library, 1974, 85–104.
———. "Mathematics and the Good." In *Science and Philosophy*. New York: Philosophical Library, 1974, 105–21.
———. *Modes of Thought*. New York: Free Press, 1938.
———. *Process and Reality: An Essay in Cosmology*, corrected edition. Edited by David Ray Griffin and Donald W. Sherburne. New York: Free Press, 1978.
———. *Religion in the Making*. New York: Fordham University Press, 1996.
———. *Science and the Modern World*. New York: Free Press, 1925.
———. *Symbolism: Its Meaning and Effect*. New York: Fordham University Press, 1955.
Wolfe, Thomas. *Look Homeward Angel*. New York: Scribner's, 1929.
Wood, Forest. "Creativity: Whitehead and Nietzsche." *Southwest Philosophical Studies* 9, no. 2 (Winter 1983): 49–59.

Index

About the Author

J. Thomas Howe is a professorial lecturer in theology at Georgetown University. He serves on the Board of Distinguished Visitors at the School of Religion at Claremont Graduate University.